ART OF FABRIC
BLOCK
PRINTING
ANDRIA GREEN
AN ILLUSTRATED GUIDE
with 12 PLAYFULLY
MODERN PROJECTS
stashBOOKS
an imprint of C&T Publishing
I0817574

PUBLISHER: Amy Barrett-Daffin

CREATIVE DIRECTOR: Gailen Runge

SENIOR EDITOR: Roxane Cerda

EDITOR: Madison Moore

TECHNICAL EDITOR: Helen Frost

COVER/BOOK DESIGNER: April Mostek

PRODUCTION COORDINATOR: Tim Manibusan

ILLUSTRATOR: Aliza Shalit

PHOTOGRAPHY COORDINATOR: Rachel Ackley

FRONT COVER AND LIFESTYLE PHOTOGRAPHY by Jasmine Rose, unless otherwise noted

INSTRUCTIONAL PHOTOGRAPHY by Andria Green, unless otherwise noted

Published by Stash Books, an imprint of C&T Publishing, Inc., P.O. Box 1456, Lafayette, CA 94549

Library of Congress Control Number: 2025019182

Printed in China

10 9 8 7 6 5 4 3 2 1

DEDICATION

TO PAUL AND CONNOR, my very best guys.
Thank you for the endless support and love.

TO GRANDMA SHIRLEY, thank you for passing on
your artistic talents. I hope you are proud up there.

TO ALL OF MY STUDENTS OVER THE YEARS,
thank you for teaching me as much as I teach you.

acknowledgments

What an incredible opportunity and learning experience this has been. Thank you to everyone who helped in the creation of this book. A special thanks especially to Madison, my editor, for her endless patience and her support of me and my ideas, and to the whole team at C&T for their hard work and creative brains.

The biggest thank you to my sweet family for all of the flexibility and understanding over the past six months while I pursued this huge step in my career. My wonderful husband Paul has been a partner I could only dream of, picking up the slack around the house, being present for our son when my brain is scrambled, and making me eat food when I get too busy and forget. I cherish you even when I am crabby, and you are my favorite person ever. My sweet son, Connor, has been so patient during this as well, sorting his trading cards and making me drawings while I work away. Thank you for your happiness and hugs and endless questions about what I am working on now. You are my very cutest and best.

Thank you to my family, including my brother, sister-in-law, amazing nieces and nephews, my in-laws, aunts, uncles, and cousins, for the love and support. I love you all!

Thank you to my students, past and present, for being some of my favorite humans. You are the best hype people an artist could ask for, and I love being inspired by your work and your kindness every week.

Thank you to all of the friends in my artistic community for the support and encouragement, for being a sounding board, for offering to help, and for believing in me. It means more than I can possibly express.

Thank you to all of my mom friends. You get the juggling of work and parenting and have supported me through all of it. I love you all.

And last but certainly not least, to The Creator. God's hand is in it all, and I will always be thankful for this beautiful world filled with endless inspiration. I can do all things through Him who strengthens me.

CONTENTS

Creating has always been something of an escape for me. It's a way to tune out the world and just make something from scratch with my own two hands. I have been creating since I was a child, finding flowers in the backyard to make into chain necklaces, or sewing little pillows for my bed. Now, as an adult, I find a mental escape in repeat printing, with its methodical process and (usually) predictable results. When I am sewing or printing, my brain can slow down and focus and be quiet for a little bit.

When I began my creative business almost a decade ago, I wanted to provide others with bright and happy things for their home. What drives me, of course, is a little deeper than that, though. Our homes are not only reflections of who we are, but of who we *want* to be each day in the world. I truly believe that surrounding ourselves with happy patterns and bright colors can affect our mood, and in turn affect how we show up in the world. This book teaches you how to create your own designs, print repeat patterns, and sew those hand-printed fabrics into cheerful home goods and accessories. But it also teaches you to celebrate the joys in imperfections, the happiness that color can bring to your life, and the beauty in everyday details.

Printmaking is one of the oldest art forms in the world. There are so many different ways to be a printmaker, from screen printing to etching to woodcut. Block printing is one of the most accessible forms, with materials that take up very little space and ink and tools that are inexpensive and easy to find. This book will introduce you to various techniques in block printing, such as rolling multiple colors at once and layering prints.

Use this book as a starting point for your block printing journey. Embrace the imperfections. Get creative with color combinations. Each project lists specific colors and blocks to achieve results similar to those pictured, but once you get the hang of the block printing process, the possibilities are endless. Combining designs to create new patterns or switching the pictured colors to something unconventional can be the most fun parts of the printmaking process. Have fun!

TOOLS AND MATERIALS

Block printing is one of the most accessible forms of printmaking because the tools and materials take up a small amount of space, and they're easy to find. Almost everything in this chapter can be found at local or large art supply stores, as well as at online retailers. Your workspace can be simple too—the majority of the projects in this book use ink that cleans up with just water and soap at your kitchen sink. Finding the right combination of brayer, ink, and block materials takes practice, but practice makes almost perfect!

BLOCK TYPES

There are so many block types for the different kinds of printmaking that it can be overwhelming. But, let's keep it simple. The best blocks to use for printing on fabric are those made out of materials like rubber, meaning they have some flexibility and give.

Speedy-Carve by Speedball is my go-to block type for fabric printing. These blocks have a slightly higher price point than Soft-Kut, but are still very affordable and can be bought in large sheets. They are a flexible, pink rubber material, similar to a pink eraser, with a smooth surface that cuts like butter. Speedy-Carve blocks can be used with oil-based inks or water-based inks with proper technique. All of the projects in this book will be printed with Speedy-Carve blocks, which you can find at Blick Art Materials, lots of local art and crafts stores, or online. If you plan to create more than a couple of projects, buying a large block of Speedy-Carve and cutting it into smaller sizes is a great and cost-effective option.

Blocks from across a decade of printmaking

Speedy-Carve blocks

Soft-Kut blocks are the easiest rubber blocks to carve and the most inexpensive to purchase. They are a great beginner block because of the low price point, and they carve smoothly. The surface is a bit slippery, making them great for even distribution with oil-based inks. I would not recommend using Soft-Kut blocks for water-based inks, as the surface is *too* slippery. Something to consider with these blocks is the longevity; because they are so flexible, they are more prone to breaking and wearing down over time.

Gray linoleum, also known as battleship linoleum, is a great option for printing on paper. It can also work well with fabric if you have a printing press that applies even pressure on the block. These blocks are thinner, less flexible, and more brittle than rubber blocks. However, they hold more detail in the carving process, and can work well for certain projects.

Gray Linoleum

CARVING TOOLS

Using the correct carving tool is essential to creating a detailed and easy to print block. High-end tools can be great, but a simple, starter carving tool with multiple carving heads works just as well and lasts for years.

speedball cutter sets

The Speedball Linoleum Cutter is the best tool for the projects in this book. It comes with five carving tips. I have been using mine since college, and have only had to replace one of the blades! In this book, we will primarily use carving tips #2 and #5. The #2 and #3 tips are V-shaped, and the #5 tip is U-shaped. The #2 tip is perfect for carving along lines, and the #5 tip is great for removing larger areas of the block. The #3 tip is also helpful for removing areas that aren't huge, but are still wider than the #2 blade. The handle is plastic, comfortable to use for long carving sessions, and has a small storage compartment in the bottom to hold all of the blades.

Be sure that, if you're using another set or carving tool, you have a variety of blades to carve different line widths and you're using a tool meant for carving rubber.

flexcut tools

If you are a more advanced block printer, or want to invest in specific blade widths for cutting, Flexcut tools are great. They have sturdy wooden handles, and there are dozens of options. I have a small set of Flexcut palm tools, and I like them for carving blocks that I will print on paper.

other cutting tools

A craft knife, like an X-Acto, is great to have around for cutting larger rubber sheets into smaller blocks. You may also consider carving on a self-healing cutting mat so that you don't damage your work surface.

BRAYERS AND ROLLERS

Brayers are used to roll ink onto carved blocks, and come in all different sizes and textures. In order to properly ink a block, the brayer should be as wide as the block. All of the projects in this book will work with a 4″ brayer. Wide brayers are helpful for creating blended ink rolls (see Printing, page 31) and small brayers are great for small, more detailed blocks.

Each texture on a brayer works with different types of ink. All of the projects in this book use a brayer with a smooth surface, which can be found at Blick Art Materials, online, or local arts and craft stores. In general, if a brayer has a smooth, non-porous surface, it will work well with oil-based inks. A porous, foam brayer works well with water-based screen printing inks.

PRINTMAKING INKS

The two main types of ink used for printmaking are *oil-based* and *water-based*. However, there are so many variations in each category that choosing the right ink for your projects can be confusing. Both types of ink come in a variety of colors, and can be mixed to create custom colors.

oil-based inks

Oil-based inks, also called fabric block printing inks, are my recommendation as you begin printing on fabric. Speedball's Fabric Block Printing Ink has been used for every project in this book.

Avoid oil-based inks that are meant for paper block printing, as those will be more difficult to clean and are typically not washable. Oil-based inks have a slight odor that can be unpleasant if you are printing for long periods of time inside your home or in a space that is not well ventilated. But, the Speedball Fabric Block Printing Inks are great for a home workspace. These inks allow you to skip heat-setting, and are thicker, making them easier to print with. Use a smooth, non-porous soft, or hard rubber brayer with oil-based inks. Drying times can vary depending on which color is used. Red ink can take up to a week to dry, while other colors can take only a day or two. However, it is best to give all of the inks in this book a week to fully dry before using or sewing with the fabric.

water-based inks

While I recommend starting with the oil-based inks described on the previous page if you're new to block printing, acrylic, water-based inks are my personal favorites to block print on fabric with. These are usually labeled as screen printing inks. They have very little smell and a relatively long *open time*—the amount of time they stay wet while printing—which helps with projects that take longer to print. However, acrylic inks can be tricky to block print with, as they are thinner and more slippery than oil-based inks. White acrylic ink is the thickest consistency of all the colors, so mixing it into the other colors can help the ink work even better for block printing. With water-based acrylic inks, cleanup is easy. You can clean your tools and workspace with just water. Porous foam brayers or smooth, soft foam brayers work best with water-based inks since the ink is thin.

***Tip:** Water-soluble inks, a subset of water-based inks, will wash out of fabric even if they are heat-set. Acrylic, screen printing, water-based inks will not wash out of fabric if they are properly heat-set. Make sure you're not working with a water-soluble ink on fabric.*

You must heat-set water-based inks if you are working on a project that will be washed, such as a towel, garment, or pillow. *Heat-setting* is the process of ironing the backside of the printed fabrics for about three minutes. Each individual brand of water-based ink comes with heat-setting instructions on the container. My favorite water-based inks are Speedball's Screen Printing Ink, and Blick's Acrylic Screen Printing Ink. Versatex and Jacquard are other brands with a much thinner consistency. I find them tricky to block print with.

ink cleanup

Before cleaning, be sure to either save or dispose of any large amounts of ink. Water- and oil-based inks can be rinsed down the drain if you are cleaning small amounts, but too much ink can clog the pipes. Be sure to wash blocks and brayers as soon as you are finished printing, as leaving ink to dry on either of those tools can ruin the surface, making it impossible to clean or print with these tools later.

For oil-based fabric inks, clean with soap and water. Put a small drop of dish soap onto your block, brayer, and ink tray, and foam it up with a soft sponge or soft bristle brush. Lay the blocks flat on a towel to dry, and lay the brayers face up so they do not get dented or stuck to any surfaces as they dry.

Tip: Saving extra ink is always better than throwing it away. Since oil-based inks often come in tubes, it's not easy to put extra ink back into the container. Try to squeeze a little out at a time, so you don't waste ink, or store any extra ink or newly mixed colors in a new container. Food containers are great for saving colors—just be sure to only use those containers for ink.

OTHER INK TOOLS

Any flat, non-porous surface will work for rolling out ink. Ink trays with a lip around the edge are great for containing any messes, but if you are careful, a flat acrylic palette or glass sheet works well. Grab a palette knife for mixing colors together. You need an ink tray for each color you're using in a printing session, as well as a separate brayer for each color. Spatulas are helpful for getting water-based ink out of containers (water-based ink usually comes in jars). The spatulas also work well for mixing ink colors. I buy mine from the kitchen section, and then use them for ink only.

Additionally, I recommend a drying rack if you're going to be printing lots of fabric. A foldable two- or three-tiered clothing drying rack works great. At minimum, you need a flat area where fabric can dry undisturbed.

FABRICS

Natural fabrics are always best for block printing, as they have a surface that easily absorbs ink, and can be heat-set and washed without issue. My favorite fabrics are cotton and linen, and these are easy to source online or at any fabric store. Be sure to avoid synthetic blends, since some fabrics may have spandex, polyester, or other blended fibers. Stretchy fabrics such as knits or jersey can be tricky to print on, as the inked blocks can stretch out the fabric as they are pulled off of the surface. Lightweight fabrics such as silk can get weighed down by the ink, so try to avoid those as well. Choose a fabric with a smooth surface and minimal texture, as this will give you the most consistent prints. I like to use prints (aka fabrics *already* designed with prints) for linings and accents. They are fun to match with the block printed fabrics for the projects in this book.

FUSIBLE STABILIZERS

Fusible stabilizers are fleece, polyester, or cotton with small glue dots covering one side of the fabric. These are great for giving printed fabrics a little more stiffness and structure. I like to use fusible interfacing and fleece when making pouches. Pellon makes great fusible stabilizers, and can be found at most craft and fabric stores, or online. We will be using fusible interfacing Pellon SF101, and fusible fleece Pellon 987f in the pouch projects in this book.

PAINTING TEXTILES

A really fun way to add detail or a pop of shimmer to hand printed textiles is textile paint. These come in many different colors, brands, and consistencies. My favorites to work with are made by Jacquard, and come in metallics and neon colors, as well as a full range of basic colors. These can be found at Blick Art Materials, or online. The Shine Bright Like a Diamond Zipper Pouch (page 90) uses Jacquard metallic paint to add detail.

OTHER HELPFUL TOOLS

I love to add a fun charm or tassel to my pouches, and you only need a few simple tools. After purchasing the add-ons online or at a craft store, find a small pair of needle nose pliers and small jump rings. Use the pliers to open up the jump ring, slide the ring onto the zipper pull, and add the charm or tassel. Use the pliers to close the ring, and you have a fun little accent on the zipper. For more, see Blobby Cosmetics Zipper Pouch (page 108).

PRINTING SURFACE

Block printing can be done just about anywhere, but it is important that you protect the surface you are printing on from ink and heat. A simple wooden or plastic folding table works great, but be mindful of any creases or texture on the table, as those will affect the quality of the prints.

Use a painting dropcloth to cover the printing area and protect it from any ink splatters or printing off the edges of the fabric. Choose a cotton dropcloth if you plan to iron on the surface as well. I like to double layer a cotton dropcloth on my printing table to give it a little padding, and I have found this helps my block prints look uniform and solid. Wearing an apron to protect your clothes is always a good idea. I have ruined so much clothing during my artistic career—it's better to always be ready for a mess!

SEWING TOOLS

Many of these projects require a sewing machine, but a simple machine with a straight stitch is all you need. For some projects, we will sew through multiple layers of fabric, so you may need heavy-duty needles (depending on the fabric you choose). The machine I use is a Juki, and I joke that I love it so much I could marry it! My Singer and Brother heavy-duty machines worked just fine in the beginning of my career, but if you sew a lot, a Juki is an amazing investment.

I almost always use a heavy-duty sewing needle, such as a 110/18. Schmetz 90/14 teflon non-stick needles are great for sewing projects that have fusible interfacing or fleece, since those can be sticky on a regular needle. Basic all-purpose thread works well for any project in this book. Sewing pins and clips will be incredibly helpful in keeping multiple layers of fabric in place. A seam ripper is also a necessity. Beyond fixing mistakes, it's used for sewing the pillowcase (see Strawberry Moon Throw Pillow, page 102), as you will need to remove stitches when you install the invisible zipper.

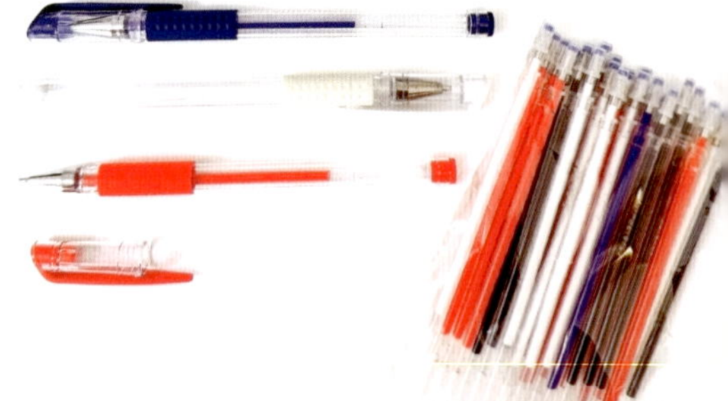

Invest in a good pair of fabric scissors. They are life-changing! Fiskars makes titanium fabric scissors that *actually have* changed my life, as I no longer get blisters from fabric cutting.

You need an iron for pressing and preparing fabric. Fabric pens are useful for planning out a printing design, or for measuring and marking fabric. My favorite pens are heat erasing pens, with ink that disappears with an iron. Outus Heat Erase Pens come in four colors, so you can choose the best option based on the color of the fabric. Find them online.

You need a ruler for measuring and cutting fabric, but a yardstick is helpful during printing to make sure the blocks are lined up straight and as desired.

SOURCING BLANK PRODUCTS FOR PRINTING

A few of the projects in this book are printed on pre-made blank products, like a tea towel or apron. I like that these products make useful block-printing projects accessible, even if you don't sew. These blank, base textiles can be found online on sites like Tote Bag Factory, Amazon, craft stores, or even Target. Some of these sites will offer discounts on large quantities if you are looking to create in bulk or sell the products you create. As always, be sure to check the descriptions online for fabric content to find natural fabrics like cotton or linen. If you prefer to use fabric you already have, you can always use your favorite pattern to sew a textile instead of purchasing a pre-made product.

DESIGN AND INSPIRATION

While this book includes templates for all the blocks used in the projects, you may want to start designing your own blocks! Inspiration can truly come from anywhere. I have found ideas for block designs while taking a walk in the forest preserve, looking at wall tiles in a church in Italy on my honeymoon, and while teaching art to first graders. Look around your home, your backyard, and your commute to work. What inspires you or brings a smile to your face? Is it sunshine coming through yellow leaves on a fall day? Is it the repeat patterns on the tiles at the train stop? Is it the colors your child used on their art project at school? The best way I have found to find inspiration is to simply stop and look around at the everyday moments and think of what brings you joy.

Just a simple glance at my personal work, as well as the patterns in this book, will tell you that my biggest inspiration is nature. There are so many ways to interpret a strawberry, one single leaf from a tree, or the pattern on your favorite blanket. (By the way, quilt blocks translate beautifully to block-printing repeat patterns!)

CREATING A REPEAT PATTERN

Repeat patterns can be printed in a number of different ways. Some repeat seamlessly when printed in a grid, with each print right next to the previous print. Other prints are a little more random and do not have elements on each edge that repeat throughout the pattern and need to be matched-up.

Seamless repeat pattern

Seamless repeat pattern

Single motif pattern

seamless repeat layouts

In a seamless repeat pattern, you can't tell exactly where one block print ends and the next begins. So, the block should have edges that line up. When drawing the design for the block, include design elements that will create new shapes or patterns when printed next to one another. For example, a triangle drawn and carved on the edge of a block will create a diamond when printed in a seamless repeat pattern. It can be really fun to see what new shapes appear when printing.

single motif layouts

Free standing elements, such as the orange and leaf pattern in the Oranges Tote Bag (page 62) and the peaches and leaves in the Just Peachy T-shirt (page 66) do not seamlessly repeat. Instead, they are repeated as individual motifs. In general, if the outside shape of a block is angular (square, rectangle, etc.), the pattern can repeat seamlessly. If the outside shape of a block is more organic (a fruit, a flower, etc.), you will be printing a freehand repeat pattern, lining up prints with your eyes or a yardstick instead of with the edge of a previous print.

DESIGNING A BLOCK

inspiration

The first step in designing a block is to decide what you will print. Food-inspired blocks are always fun for kitchen items like aprons, tea towels, and oven mitts. Nature-inspired blocks can be great for clothing, totes, and home decor. One of my block designs features a mountain and sunshine scene inside the pages of a book. I love using this block for tote bags because it fits well with carrying library books or school supplies! Matching the block to its use can really enhance the block printed design.

A block with simple geometric shapes works great with a bold color and repeat pattern printing. A floral pattern can be really beautiful for a pillow or thrifted shirt, and works well for mixing with moons, leaves, or other nature inspired shapes. Pick a general theme, and then brainstorm what elements and printing subjects fit well with that theme.

drawing a repeat block

Grid or graph paper is your best friend when designing and drawing a block. Because block printing on fabric is largely a print-and-repeat process, blocks are easier to use when they repeat seamlessly. Using grid paper simplifies creating symmetrical drawings and patterns, and when the edges of a block are symmetrical, the pattern prints repeatedly more easily. You can transfer graphite drawings from paper directly to the block by rubbing the drawing onto the rubber. You don't have to worry as much about symmetry if you're making a non-repeating, single-motif block.

scale and block size

Sheets of Speedy-Carve come as large as 11¾″ x 11¾″ squares. I have carved a few blocks this large so that there's room to add lots of detail, but they can be unwieldy to line up for repeat patterns. It's difficult to get an even print every time with a large surface area. But, if you do want to make a large block, choose larger items like towels and aprons. If you choose to use a smaller fabric product with a larger block, you'll lose some elements of the block's design. There's no limit to how small you can carve a block, especially if you're layering in a small detail!

color decisions

Choose a color scheme for your project based on the design and the fabric. Bright colors work well with bold and fun patterns, while lighter colors are better for delicate florals and nature-inspired patterns. White and pastel inks work with dark fabrics, and primary colors or bright inks work with light fabrics.

My best advice is to have fun with colors! There are no right or wrong combinations, and the more you practice, the more confident you will be in making color choices that feel like you. If you create a design or pattern with multiple colors, each color will need its own block. For example, if you are printing a flower with a stem, the block for the flower will be inked with one color, and a separate block for the stem will be inked with a second color. The only exception to this rule are Rainbow Rolls (page 32) which use multiple ink colors on one block to create a gradient.

Layering colors is also a great way to create depth in a pattern. Allow oil-based inks to fully dry before layering one color on top of another.

LEARN TO BLOCK PRINT

Here we go! You are ready to start carving and printing. Be patient with yourself, and have some scrap fabric ready to test carved blocks on. It may take a few (or more) tries to get the inking process correct, but keep at it, and you will be thrilled with the results!

Block Printing Toolkit

Every block printing project will use the same basic toolkit. For more details, refer back to Tools and Materials (page 8), or or reference this section for a quick list:

- Rubber cutting blocks (Speedy-Carve)
- Cutter tool(s) with multiple tips
- Preferred fabric-printing ink (all projects in this book use Speedball Oil-Based Fabric Block Printing Ink)
- Cotton or linen fabric
- Graphite pencil
- Grid or printer paper

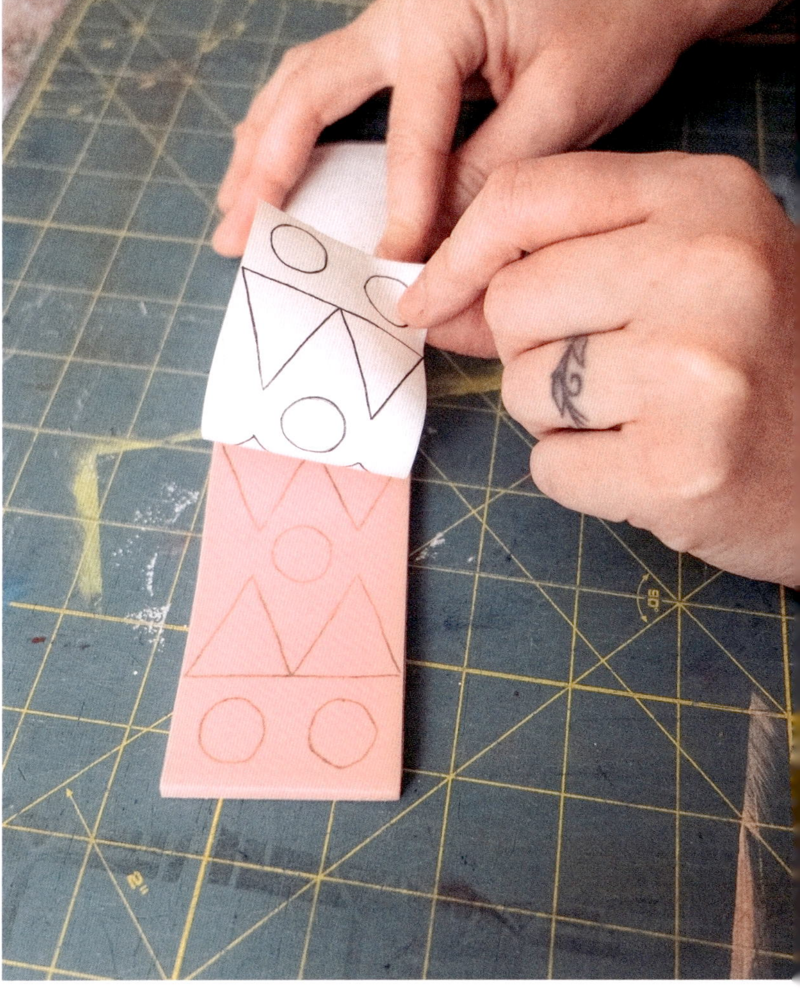

TRANSFERRING DESIGNS

This transfer method allows you to print a design exactly as you drew it. When you first transfer the drawing directly from paper to block, the design will be reversed. For example, if you draw a strawberry on the left of the design and a banana on the right, when transferred to the block using this method, the strawberry will be on the right and the banana on the left. But, when you print the block, the design will appear as it was originally drawn. So, with this transfer method, you don't have to worry about reversing or mirroring a design (like letters) when drawing it onto a block.

how to transfer a design

Transfer a template or draw a simple design onto a practice block so you can try each step of the process! An easy design to start with is the Triangles and Circles block.

1 Draw or trace the block design onto a piece of printer paper or grid paper with a graphite pencil. To access the block designs in this book, see Templates (page 124). The paper should not be thicker than printer paper, or the transferring process may be more difficult.

2 Flip the drawing so that it is pencil side down on top of the Speedy-Carve block. Line it up with an edge of the block. Scribble all over the blank back of the paper with the pencil. Fully cover the back of the sheet, so that you draw over every line of the design. You can lift up the paper on one corner occasionally to check if the pattern is fully transferring, but do not lift the paper completely off of the block until you are finished transferring the entire image.

Tip: I like to buy 11¾″ × 11¾″ Speedy-Carve square blocks even though my designs are much smaller. I transfer the design to the large sheet, then cut around the outside of each block design with a craft knife, saving the rest for the next project.

CARVING BLOCKS

carving safely

Safety first! Speedy-Carve is one of the easiest blocks to carve, but carving tools can still slip and cut your fingers. Always carve on a surface that you don't mind getting nicked, like a healing cutting mat. Always carve away from your body and your fingers. Turn the block as you carve lines and spaces, so that the carving tip is always pointed away from your body as you push it through the block.

positive and negative space

Understanding positive and negative space is crucial for carving a block. Positive space is the area of a block that is not carved, remaining smooth. Positive space is what will print. Negative space refers to any lines or areas that are carved away. If you carve away an area or line, it will not be inked and will not appear when printed. If you're using this book's templates, you should carve away all black lines and gray areas. These are the negative spaces.

carving basics

1 Start with the #2 blade in the tool. Hold the carving tool in your dominant hand, and lay the block flat on the table or cutting surface, using your other hand to keep it still.

2 Carve all the lines of the design. Holding the blade almost parallel to the surface of the block, push the bottom sharp edge of the tip into the line, and move the tool along the line, carving it away. Push the tip about ⅛″ into the surface of the block to carve all the lines of the design.

2

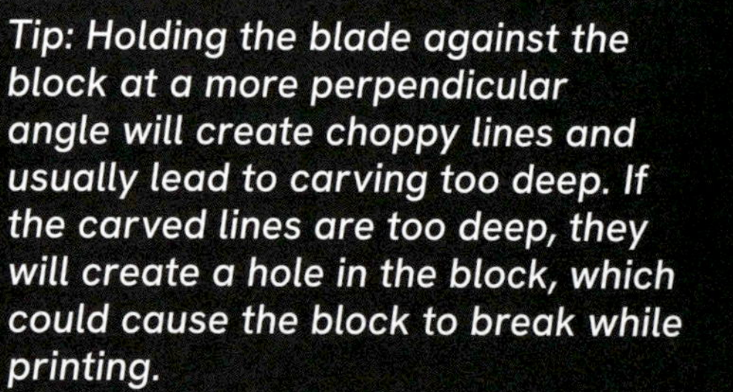

Tip: Holding the blade against the block at a more perpendicular angle will create choppy lines and usually lead to carving too deep. If the carved lines are too deep, they will create a hole in the block, which could cause the block to break while printing.

3 When the lines of the entire design are carved, use #3 and #5 blades for the rest of the negative space. Carve away the rubber around any individual motifs, and around the edges of the design/block. Anything not carved away will print. Carve backgrounds and negative space a little deeper, a little less than ¼″ deep, so that they don't pick up any ink as you are inking the block.

3

CUT AWAY EXCESS

It will make printing easier if you cut away any excess material around the block design with a craft knife. You'll notice most of my finished blocks are not simple squares or rectangles. Cut around the outside of the design, about ⅛″ from the positive spaces.

If the carved image does not have a simple square or rectangle silhouette, such as a flower or vine, using a craft knife to carve away any excess block around the silhouette is helpful. This will make it easier to see the edges of the block when it is flipped over, carved side down, for printing, and will help with registration as well.

LEAVING TABS FOR CLEAN PRINTING

As you begin practicing the printing process, you will notice you're getting very inky fingers. Everyone knows what color I printed with on any given day because it is all over my hands and under my nails! But, you can avoid some inky messiness by leaving tabs on the blocks when carving and cutting.

To do this, carve a small area outside of the design that you don't cut away. Make sure it's carved low enough that it doesn't print. Hold on to this small area of the block when flipping it over and lining it up on the fabric.

PREPARING TO INK

All of the ink used in this book is Speedball Fabric Block Printing Ink. Each color I use is listed in each project, but feel free to switch color choices or mix custom colors. These inks are oil-based, so they will dry more slowly than water-based inks. Make sure you prepare a flat area or drying rack for the printed fabrics to dry. Make sure you have enough ink trays for the number of colors you're using. Lay out the fabric or textile flat in your printing workspace.

mixing colors

The projects in this book only use colors directly from the tube, but mixing custom colors can be a great way to incorporate unique color palettes into your work. To mix colors, squeeze a small amount of each color onto an ink tray. Using a palette knife, swirl the colors around until they blend. As you print some of the projects in this book, feel free to try out custom colors of your own.

using the ink

If the project only uses one color of ink, squeeze the ink out of the tube in a line about the same length as the brayer. If the project uses a rainbow roll (see Rainbow Rolls, page 32), squeeze a small drop of each color in a line.

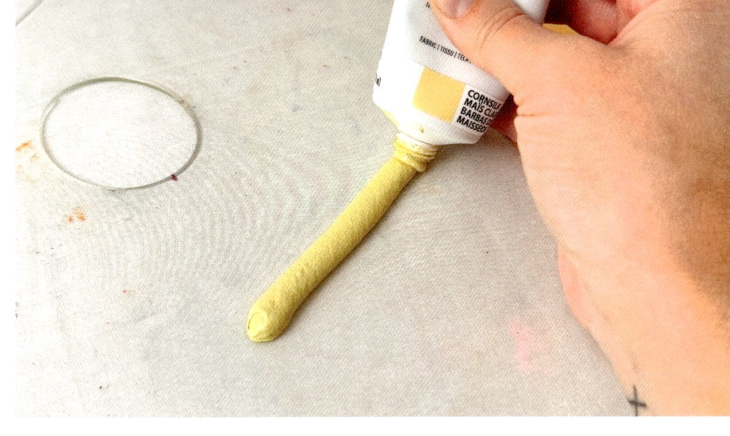

KEEPING INK FRESH

Oil-based inks don't dry out too fast while you're printing, but try to only squeeze out the amount needed for each project. The openings in the tubes of ink are small, so it will be difficult to put back any extra ink. When ink becomes too sticky, is difficult to roll, or is filling in the carved lines on the block, the ink may be drying out. Use a spatula or palette knife to scrape the old ink off the tray, and start again with a new squeeze of ink.

1

2

PRINTING

inking the block

1 Dip the brayer in the line or dots of ink on the tray. About an inch below where you squeezed out the ink, begin rolling the brayer. Roll the brayer over the ink tray until the entire surface of the brayer is evenly coated. Lift the brayer between each roll so that the ink can reach the entire surface of the cylinder.

2 When the brayer is evenly covered in ink, ink the block. Begin rolling the brayer in the middle of the block, then roll ink down to the bottom edge. Lift the brayer, and roll from the middle toward the top edge. Continue rolling all over the block, lifting the brayer up fully between each roll, until the whole block is evenly covered in ink.

3 Carefully place the brayer back on the tray in the rectangle of rolled-out ink.

4 Re-ink the block every time you print a new impression.

RAINBOW ROLLS

Rainbow rolls use two or three colors of ink on one brayer for one block. A rainbow roll is successful if the colors work and blend well together. Colors that are next to each other on the color wheel typically create nice rainbow rolls.

However, you can also create a rainbow roll with colors that may normally clash by adding white ink between them (see Blobby Cosmetics Zipper Pouch, page 108). Purple and green mix to create a muddy color, but when white is added in the middle, it keeps the colors from mucking each other up. Try different color combinations to see what looks fun together!

1 Squeeze 2–3 drops of ink onto the ink tray adjacent to one another. Dip the brayer into all of the colors at once.

2 Follow Step 1 in Inking the Block (page 31) to coat the brayer in the ink. Make sure to roll the brayer parallel with the ink tray edges so that the colors form a distinct gradient.

3 Roll with the block in the same orientation each time you ink the block so the same colors are rolled on the same areas.

4 If the block you are working with is wider than the brayer, such as the block used for the Rainbow Sun Tea Towel (page 56), ink the block in halves. Use the brayer with the magenta ink rolled on the middle of the block and the yellow on the outer edge of the block. Carefully flip the block 180 degrees, and ink the other half the same way, with the magenta meeting in the middle.

1

2A

2B

4

printing with multiple colors

When printing repeat patterns with two or more blocks and colors, assign each block a different color for that project. In some cases, the blocks will all be printed in one printing session, and sometimes you will print each color in separate sessions, allowing the ink to fully dry between printings. In general, if the prints are next to one another, they can be printed in one session.

Printing ink colors on top of one another is a really great way to add depth and interest to the fabric. If they are layered or one block is printed inside another block (see Floral Vines Bandana, page 78), wait until the first color is fully dry (about a week) to prevent colors from transferring or smearing.

flipping the block

This is where those tabs we carved earlier will come in handy! Using the tips of your fingers, hold the edges of the block on the tabs. Pick up the left edge of the block with your right hand, and the right edge of the block with your left hand. Flip the block over so that the ink is facing down (still in your hands).

printing the block

When the block is properly aligned where you want to print it, place it gently onto the fabric. Using your palms, press firmly on the back of the block, making sure to press on the entire surface of the block.

Tip: Check your fingertips before you begin pressing on the back of the block. Inky fingers could mess up the fabric as you print.

Peel the block away from the fabric. Hold the fabric flat with one hand, and peel away the edge of the block with the other hand, again pinching the tab. Work slowly so that your hands don't get messy and the print doesn't smear.

Tip: A majority of the printed patterns in this book will also need to be printed off the edges of the fabric. Make sure the printing surface you are working on is covered and protected (see Tools and Materials, page 8). You can also add a piece of scrap paper on the edge of the fabric to catch the part of the block that doesn't fit on the fabric.

registration

Each project, based on the shape of the textile and block, will have a different way of aligning, or *registering*, the blocks as you print to make a repeat pattern. However, there are a few consistent ways of registering a block and printing a repeat pattern. Practice the following methods on scrap pieces of fabric, so you can get the hang of different printing methods before diving into the projects in this book. Quilting cotton or cotton muslin are great for practice printing.

rulers and tape

Yardsticks and rulers are helpful tools for printing a design in straight rows. Make the first print, and then, with the block still on the fabric, line up the bottom of the ruler with the top of the block. As you print down the row, align the top edge of the block with the bottom edge of the ruler. You can also do this with a piece of tape instead of a ruler.

registering multiple blocks

Some projects in this book will require multiple ink colors. Some will be layered, and will need more than one printing session. Others will require registering the blocks next to or near each other as you print. This means you will use either measurements or freestyle to line up the different blocks to create a multicolored pattern.

aligning multiple blocks

If you need to align two distinct blocks, like a stem and a flower (see Tulips Table Runner, page 96), do so by marking the back of the blocks. Use a permanent marker to mark where and how the two blocks should align, then use the marks to consistently align the designs while you print.

PRINTING REPEAT PATTERNS

There are lots of different ways to repeat print a block-printed pattern. Prepare the printing method before you begin to ink the block.

> *Tip: For all measured printing methods, if you prefer, you can use a fabric pen to mark the grid lines as shown. Measure and mark, then print the block using the lines instead of referring to the ruler as you print.*

measured straight grid printing

This method of repeat printing is one you will use the most in this book. This method works best for pieces of fabric that are square or rectangle with a 90 degree corner to start printing along. It is used for single motif blocks that don't need to overlap or meet at the edges. You need a ruler. For this example, I'm using the block from the Noodles Apron (page 52).

1 Measure the block you are using. The noodles block measures 6″ wide and 3″ tall.

2 Lay a ruler along the bottom edge of the fabric, with the left end of the yardstick lined up with the left edge of the fabric.

3 Ink the block, and flip it over, lining it up with the bottom left corner of the fabric. Place the block ink side down, and print it.

4 Re-ink the block, and using the ruler as a guideline, print again with the left edge of the block aligned with the 6″ mark on the ruler and the bottom of the block aligned with the bottom of the fabric.

5 Repeat Steps 3-4, each time aligning the next print 6″ from the left side of the previous print.

1

3

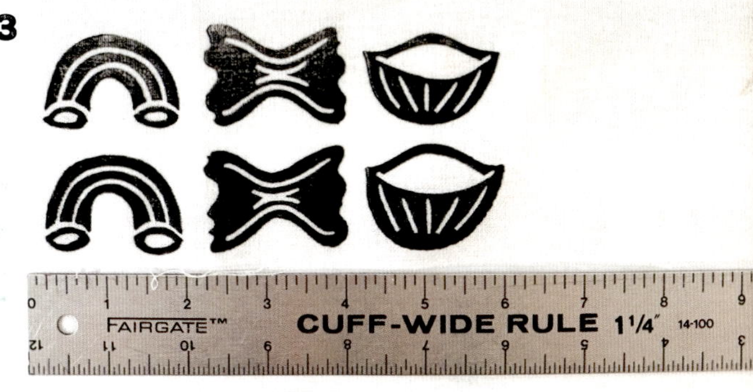

4

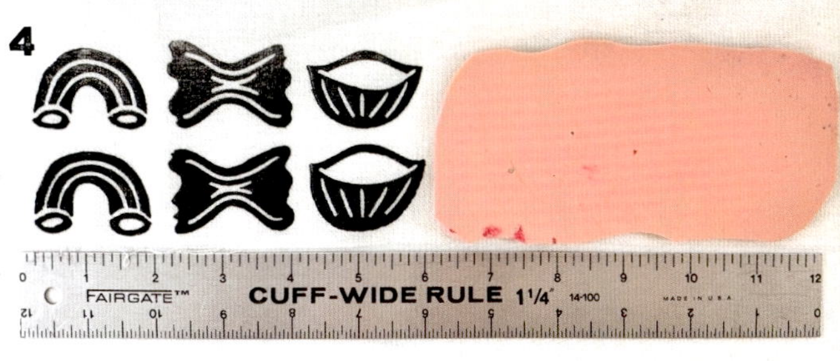

6 If the ruler is not long enough, move the left edge of the ruler to align with the left edge of the newest print. Repeat until you reach the right edge of the fabric.

7 Move the ruler to the vertical edge of the fabric at the bottom left corner. Begin the next row by aligning the block 3″ above the bottom edge of the fabric. Align the block directly above the prints in the first row.

8 Repeat Steps 3–4 to print the second row with the ruler along the bottom edge of the fabric. Repeat Step 7 any time you want to begin a new row. Print until the fabric is covered.

measured overlap straight grid printing

Use this method of straight grid printing for design elements that should meet when they're printed, creating new shapes or patterns where they intersect. You need two rulers. For this example, I am using the block from the Moon Phases Quilted Placemats (page 84).

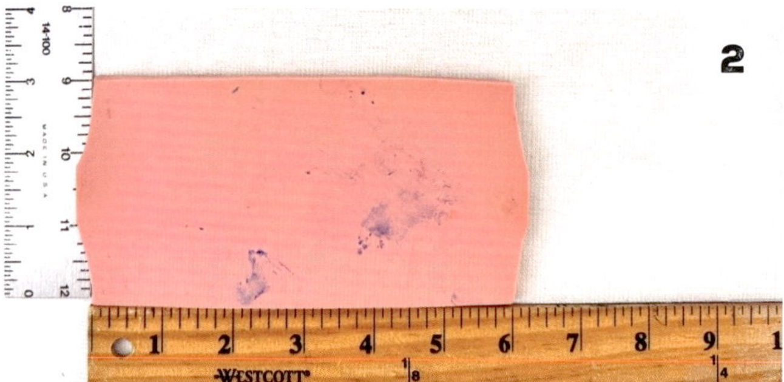

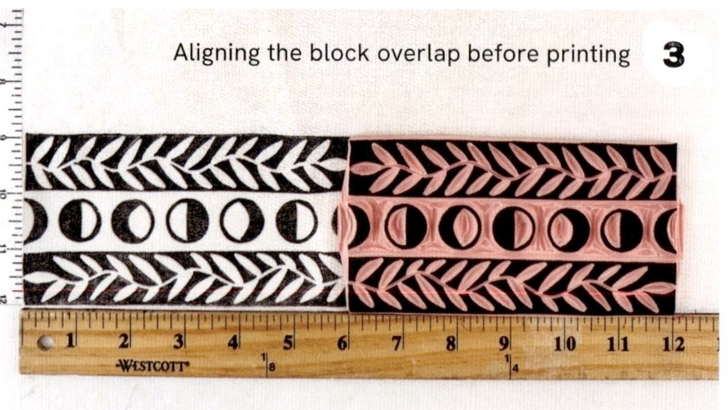

Aligning the block overlap before printing

1 Measure the block you are using. The moon phases block measures 6″ wide and 3″ tall. Place a ruler on each axis of the fabric (one vertically and one horizontally).

2 Ink the block, and flip it over, lining it up with the bottom left corner of the fabric. Place the block ink side down, and print it.

3 Re-ink the block, and using the ruler as a guideline, print again, barely overlapping the first print at the 6″ mark on the ruler and keeping the bottom of the block aligned with the bottom edge of the fabric.

4 Repeat Steps 2–3, with each print meeting the previous one, 6″ from the left edge of the previous print. Repeat until you reach the right edge of the fabric.

5 Begin the next row by aligning the block 3″ above the bottom edge of the fabric. Align the block directly above the prints in the first row. Print the block, slightly overlapping the first print.

6 Repeat Steps 2–3 to print the second row. Repeat Step 5 any time you want to begin a new row. Print until the fabric is covered.

measured staggered grid printing

Offsetting the prints is a great way to vary a pattern. For this example, I am using the block from the Blobby Cosmetics Zipper Pouch (page 108).

1 Measure the block you are using. This block measures 3″ wide and 3″ tall. Place a ruler on each axis of the fabric (one vertically and one horizontally).

2 Ink and print the first row following Steps 3–6 in Measured Straight Grid Printing (page 37).

3 To begin the second row, measure 1½″ (half the block width) from the left edge of the fabric. Then, measure 3″ from the bottom of the fabric. Print with the left edge of the block aligned with the 1½″ mark.

4 Print the rest of the row that fits on the fabric, repeating Step 2 to place the prints every 3″.

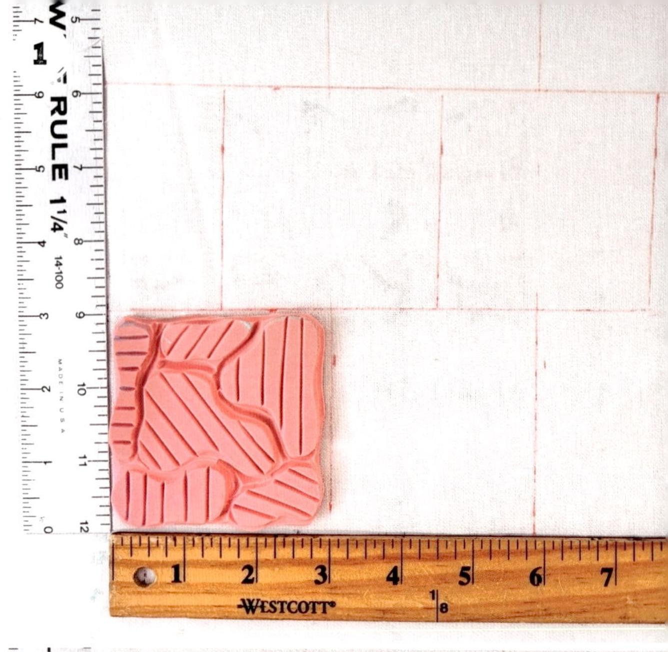

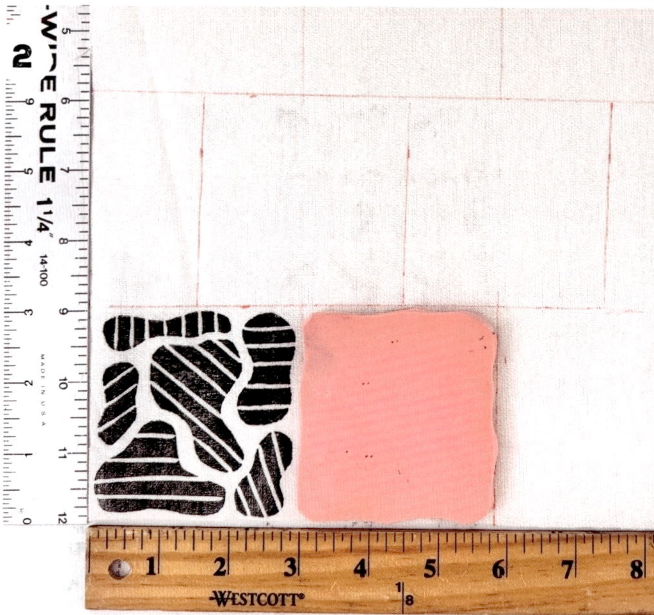

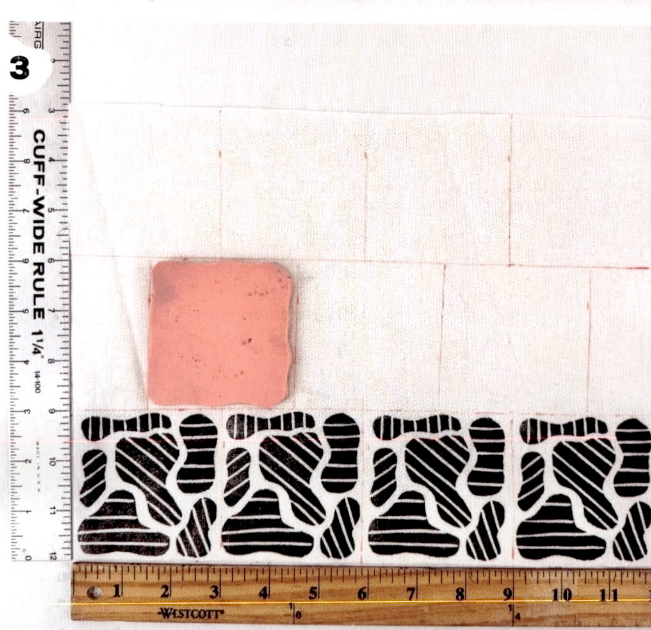

5

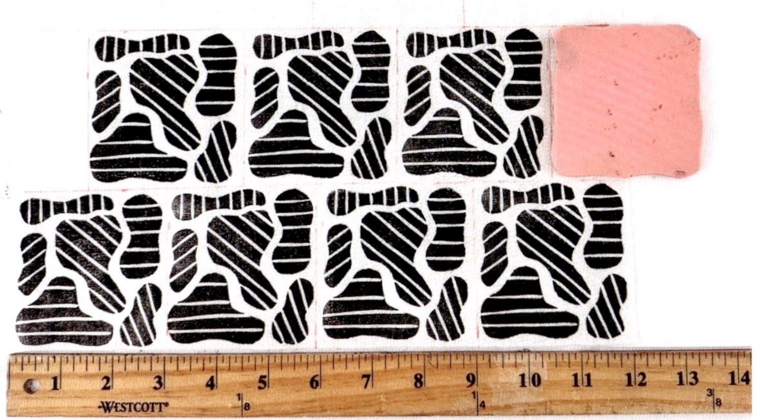

5 Print half the block on the left and right edges of the row, making sure there is a scrap fabric or paper to protect your work surface.

6

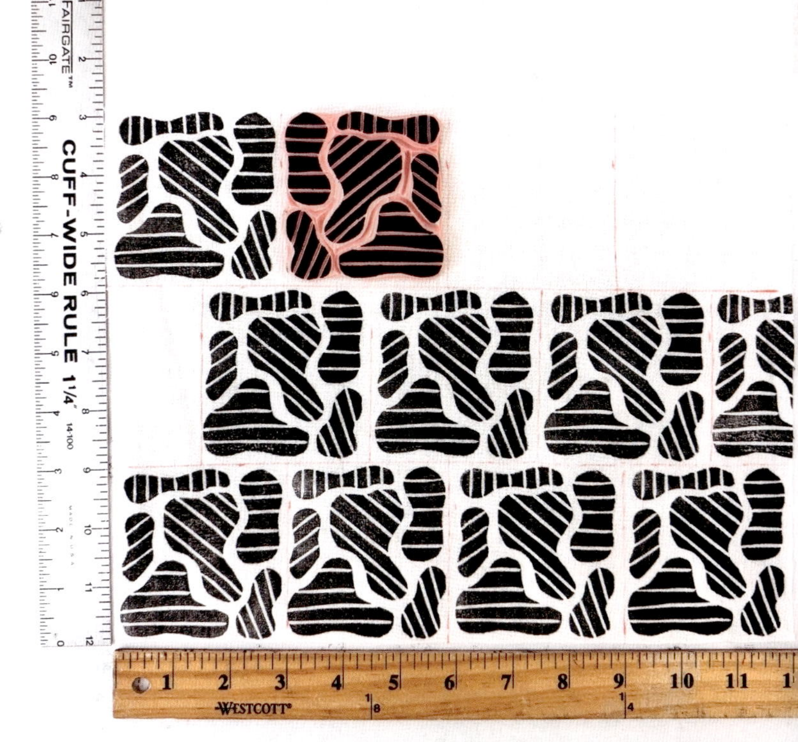

6 Print the third row aligned with the first row, moving up 3″ and repeating Step 2. Continue staggering every other row until the fabric is fully printed.

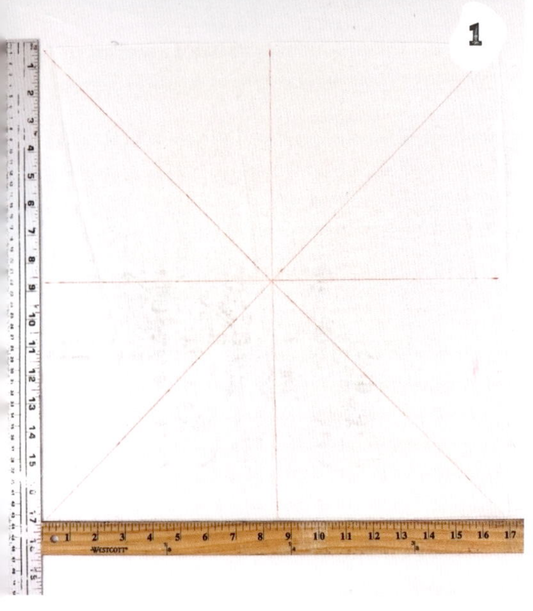

symmetrical pattern printing

This method of printing works great for printing with multiple colors and printing a square or rectangular shaped product such as a tote bag or bandana. It has elements of measured printing and freestyle printing. You can choose where you want to print the blocks, but always make sure they are symmetrically placed on the guidelines. For this example, I am using blocks from the Floral Vines Bandana (page 78).

1 Using a ruler and fabric pen, divide the fabric into quarters with straight lines. Then, draw a line from corner to corner across both diagonals.

2 Print the stripes block, centered and about ¼″ from the edge, on each of the 4 quadrant lines. Note that I marked the halfway point on the block so I can align it with the quadrant lines.

3 Measure and mark 7″ from each corner along the diagonal lines. Print the flower block on each of the four lines, centered.

freestyle repeat patterns

This method of printing requires a little eyeballing, and a lot of patience with yourself. Freestyle printing is great with patterns that are single motifs. For this example, I'm using the blocks from the Just Peachy T-Shirt (page 66).

A great way to practice an intuitive skill like this is to be able to move the prints around. So, I suggest using an ink stamp pad and paper to create moveable prints before you begin to print on fabric. If you don't have an ink stamp pad meant to be used on paper, you can also draw the design a few times instead.

1 Print the peach block on a piece of paper using the ink stamp pad. Rinse and dry the block. Print 8–10 times, filling the page.

2 Cut out each print, and then lay the pieces of paper out on the fabric. Play around with spacing, adding more cutouts, or even measuring space between cutouts if you want a more consistent pattern. Rotate the prints in different orientations.

3 Once you're satisfied with the placement, prepare the block with fabric-printing ink. Print each spot where you placed a paper cutout.

Tip: You don't have to arrange paper prints every time you freestyle print, but it's a great way to figure out how you want a print to look before you commit! If you feel confident or bold, you can also freestyle print directly onto fabric.

CARING FOR BLOCK PRINTED TEXTILES

One of the best things about printing your own textiles is creating useful and wearable pieces. However, apparel and kitchen projects will need to be cleaned occasionally. Because the inks used in this book are permanent, machine washing is an easy way to care for your handmade things. Machine wash using a delicate cycle and fragrance-free detergent. Line dry to preserve the ink for as long as possible.

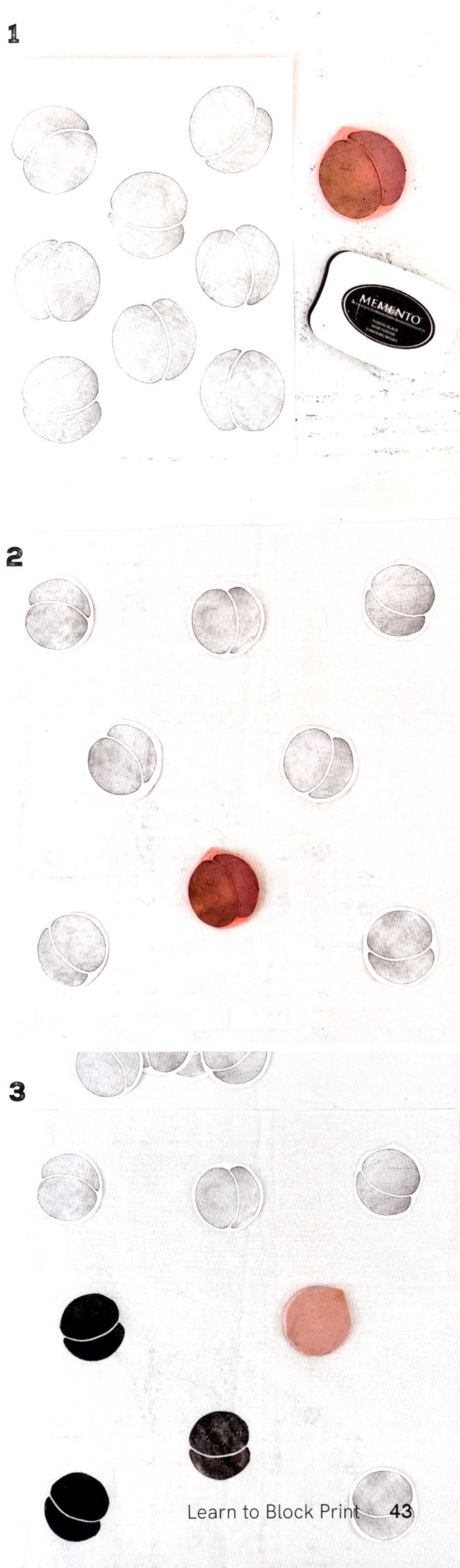

RUNNING A CREATIVE BUSINESS

My creative block printing business began just about ten years ago. I always knew my brain and my body were not made for a traditional 9-5 work environment. Finding any and all ways to make a living as an artist has been a fulfilling, but sometimes exhausting, journey. Starting a business isn't the first thing you should think of when you start a new craft. Finding your creative voice is a big part of the journey, and making sure others hear that voice comes after. But if you're ready to start selling your work, this chapter will help start you on your way.

Please note that the designs, templates, and projects in this book are for personal use only. If you wish to start printing and selling your own work (which I encourage you to try if you're interested!), make sure you are using your own original block designs, prints, and products.

MARKETING YOUR WORK

If no one knows your work exists, no one can buy it. The good news is that there are endless free marketing tools at your disposal. If you have a smartphone, you are able to start marketing your work. Consider what makes your work unique, why you feel that customers need it, and create a plan to start sharing your products.

social media

Social media is the fastest and cheapest way to get your work seen in the world. Sites like Instagram have made creating a curated online presence easy and free. Simply create a business account, look at possible hashtags that represent your work, and start posting regularly. A great way to catch attention on social media is to ensure you have a unique style or curated posts. Are your patterns inspired by folk art and whimsy? Or are they more bold and modern? Think about the colors you use on a regular basis, and try to use them regularly in your posts. I've found that a curated feed is more likely to attract customers who are interested in my work.

email newsletters

It can sometimes be difficult to be seen on social media, so a surefire way to reach your customers is to create an email newsletter. This can be done through various sites; mine is through my Wix website. Ask friends and family who are interested in your work to sign up, and always bring a sign up sheet to events you participate in. While your audience may be more slow-growing than on social media, you can reach the people on your email list more directly, keeping your work in front of them.

word of mouth

Probably the oldest and still most effective form of marketing is telling people about your work! Those people tell more people, and so on. Some of my regular customers found me through a friend who purchased from me. Try to keep business cards on you; you never know when you will meet someone who needs a new table runner or wants custom linens for their event. Create beautiful, well-made work, and customers will tell their friends and family about you.

STREAMS OF REVENUE

I give this advice to all small art businesses: Do not put all of your eggs in one basket. Streams of revenue ebb and flow all the time. Income can be dependent on the economy, where you live, or even trends in decor and art. Diversifying how you bring in money can help pick up the slack when some areas are slower.

online retail

Etsy is a great starting point for makers and artists who want to sell their work. Setting up a shop is easy, uploading photos and adding descriptions to products is quick, and you can create shipping labels on their site. They do take a percentage of your profits for processing fees, listing fees, and shipping, but it is a huge marketplace that has a loyal following, so it'll also help you discover new customers.

Creating your own website is a great option for when you have established your business a bit more. Sites like Shopify or Squarespace are also easy to build a platform on, and you can send email newsletters directly from those sites. You may not have the same traffic to your site as Etsy would bring in, but this is where those marketing skills will come in handy, and you get to keep more of your profit!

shows and markets

I live in Chicago, so every single weekend there seems to be at least five craft and art events happening. But even if you aren't in a big city, you can still find local events to sell your work at. Different shows cater to different types of makers. Some are specific to a medium (pottery, fiber arts, etc.) and some like to offer variety. Social media is a great way to find these events, or you can ask local makers and artists for recommendations.

Large events charge larger booth fees, typically hundreds of dollars, but in exchange, they advertise the makers' work on their social media pages, and bring in large crowds of customers. Smaller events are cheaper to participate in, but bring in smaller crowds. Consider the price points of your work and how much money you would need to make up to cover the booth fee before applying to a show. Sometimes it takes a few tries with an event to decide if it is right for your business or not.

My booth at a craft fair

Selling your work at a fair or market has a few advantages that selling online can lack. The biggest advantage is meeting customers face to face. There are few things as rewarding as seeing someone's face light up when they connect with your work. Sharing your products and inspiration can create lasting relationships with customers, who will continue to support your business throughout the years. Another perk of selling at a market is figuring out who your target audience is. Social media can provide some of this information (for example, my key audience tends to be women ages 25–44). Meeting customers at events and seeing who purchases your work can be helpful for how you market your products and which shows you participate in. Another advantage for me as a textile maker is allowing customers to see and feel the quality of my work. These things can be difficult to convey through online photos, so giving people the opportunity to see the colors and pick up the products and feel the fabrics is helpful for making sales.

wholesale

Selling your work wholesale is a way to sell directly to stores and small shops. They purchase your work at a lower price (typically half of the retail price), but they purchase the work in bulk.

This is a great way to get your work in front of more people, especially if the shops you work with are in a different city or state. Wholesale buying often ebbs and flows with retail sales. The first few months of every year are the slowest for retail sales. However, these same months are when shops begin buying products for the spring holidays (such as Mother's Day and Easter), so wholesaling at this time can be a great way to bring in income during an otherwise slow season.

You can also work with a shop on a consignment model. In this agreement, when you send a shop your products, you don't receive money until they sell your work to a customer. Each model works for different businesses, so trying both may help you decide what works best for you. I prefer wholesale to consignment, as it gives me all of the money upfront to invest back into my business.

Building wholesale connections is an important part of selling, and can be done in a few different ways. Cold calls (or emails) can occasionally work, but shops are typically too busy to respond to these. I have found over the years that emailing, reaching out, and sending samples is not the best way to build wholesale connections since shop owners have so many small businesses that reach out to them. I've personally found the most success in presenting my work clearly, and then allowing shop owners to find me. Invest in professional product photography if you can, be sure that online product descriptions are clear and concise, and have lead times (how long it will take to fill an order) clearly directed toward wholesale accounts.

design work

If you work in an illustration or design craft like block printing, designing patterns to be used digitally and selling your work through a third-party website can be a great way to make some passive income. Sites like Spoonflower or Society6 allow you to put digital pattern designs onto physical, print-to-order products from shower curtains to bedding.

WORK/LIFE BALANCE

Is there such a thing as work/life balance? Some days it certainly doesn't feel like it. But then I remind myself that building and running a small business has allowed me to spend summers with my child, take on a part-time teaching job, and, most importantly, work in my socks and pajamas. I love that this work style gives me freedom in my schedule. But, it also means it can be hard to keep a distinct boundary between my life and my work.

I would be lying if I said that running a small art business doesn't come with guilty feelings and days of overwhelm and exhaustion. But the longer you work at creating and making a living from your creations, the easier it will be to figure out what to prioritize and what to say *no* to. Some days, getting a wholesale order in the mail and having frozen pizza for dinner is the balance. Other days, logging out of social media so you can spend an uninterrupted day at the beach with your family is so much more important. Practice your boundaries, and remember what I always say to myself: There is no such thing as a tea towel emergency!

PROJECTS

The projects in this book will help you to practice all the block printing basics we covered in Learn to Block Print (page 24) while crafting a gorgeous accessory or decor project, step by step. While you're welcome to create these textiles exactly as I've designed them, as you grow more comfortable, try branching out in color, block design, or pattern! Every project requires your basic Block Printing Toolkit (page 24). All sewing projects in this book use a ¼″ seam allowance. When using the block carving templates (page 124), carve away all black lines and gray areas.

NOODLES APRON

Noodles are everyone's favorite! Ramen, ravioli, mac and cheese—there's no going wrong. There is also no going wrong with gifting your favorite chef or host this noodle apron. Plus, if you're more of an eater than a cook, these are noodles you can successfully make!

Materials

Blank cotton apron

Speedball Fabric Block Printing Ink in Cornsilk

Speedy-Carve block at least 6″ × 3″

Brayer

Ink tray

Iron

Yardstick or ruler

Masking or painter's tape

Noodles block template (see Templates, page 124)

PICKING AN APRON

Choosing a blank cotton apron that's pre-sewn saves you a lot of time on a project like this. Retailers like Amazon or Etsy have great choices. Look for something that's 100% cotton, and I suggest omitting a pocket so that you can smoothly print across the whole thing. If your apron does have a pocket, think about how best incorporate it into the print design.

PRINT THE APRON

1 Machine wash the apron to remove any starch or residue. This will help the ink to adhere to the fabric. Iron the apron flat, and place it on the work surface. If the whole apron doesn't fit, start with the bottom of the apron flat and the bodice folded at the top of the table.

2 Transfer the Noodles block template to the Speedy-Carve block (see Transferring Designs, page 25). Carve the block (see Carving Blocks, page 27).

3 Squeeze the ink onto the tray. Dip the brayer in the ink, and then roll it on the tray just below the ink dot. Continue rolling until the entire brayer is covered, lifting it between each roll. Roll the ink onto the carved block (see Inking the Block, page 31).

3

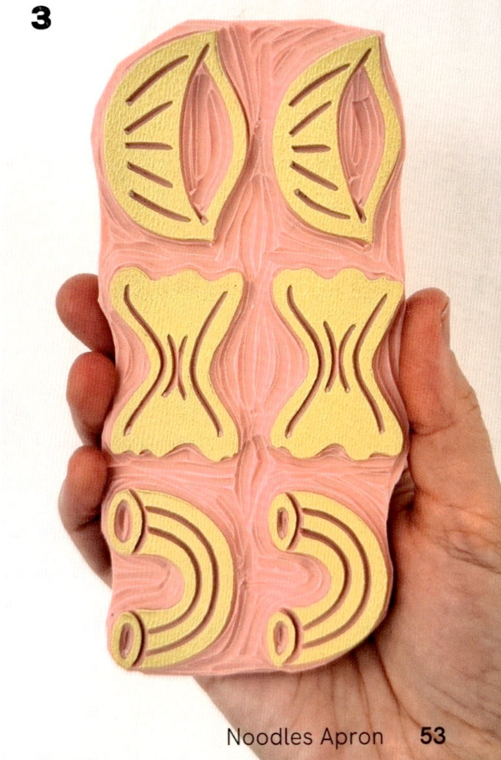

4 Line up the block with the bottom left corner of the apron, right against the bottom edge. Print the block (see Printing, page 31).

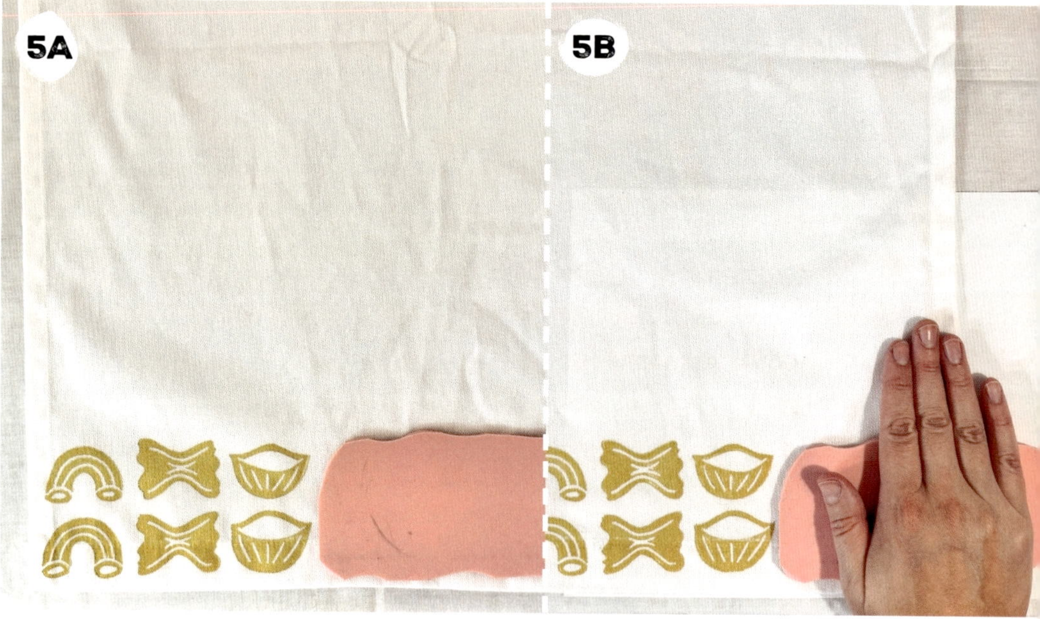

5 Print the first row using the Measured Straight Grid Printing method (page 37). This block measures 6″ wide and 3″ tall. Print off the edge of the apron if needed, making sure you are printing on a protected surface.

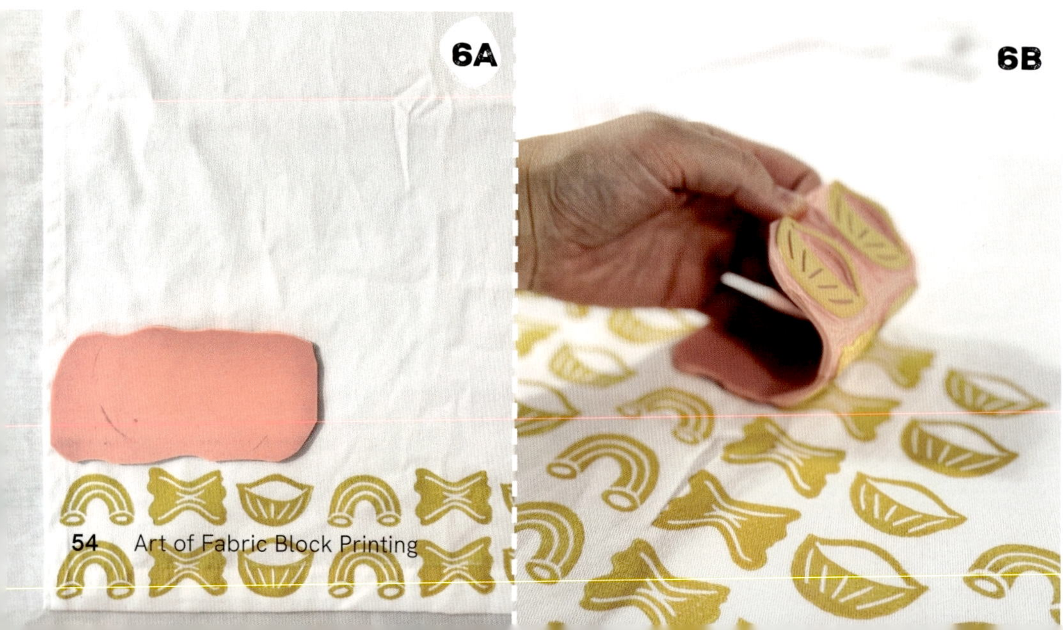

6 Start a new row, continuing to print using the same method until the flat area of the apron is covered. Again, print off the edge of the apron as needed.

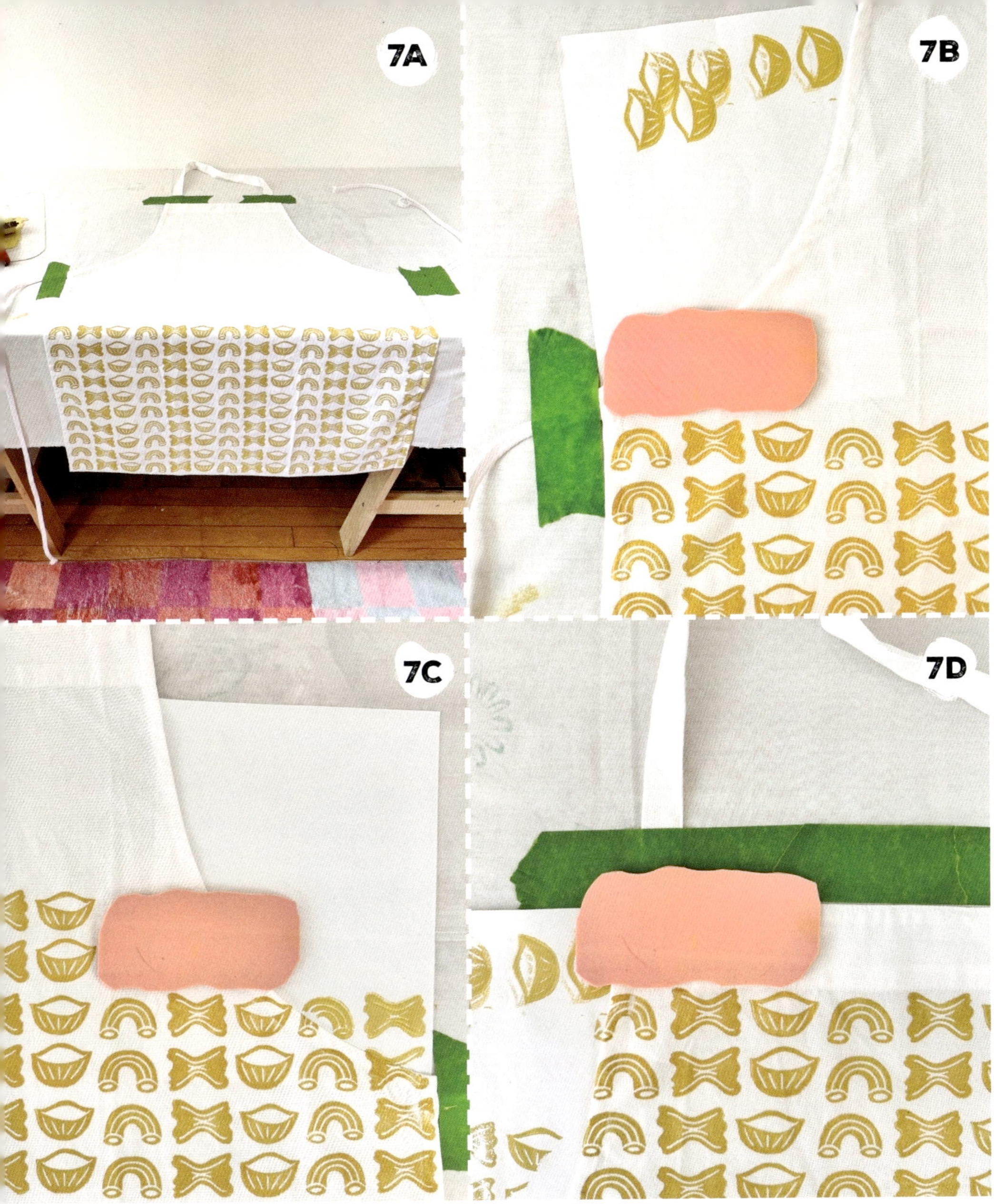

7A

7B

7C

7D

7 Move the apron up on the work surface so the bodice is flat. Use the masking tape to tape off the tie strings and neck ties, and to secure the apron to the table. Continue printing (repeating Steps 5–6), to cover the bodice. Print off the edges at the top and armholes.

8 Allow the ink to fully dry (about 1 week), and remove the tape from the ties. Machine wash on a cold delicate cycle. Tumble dry on low heat.

RAINBOW SUN TEA TOWEL

Tea towels are one of the easiest ways to jazz up a kitchen! They are versatile and useful, while also bringing color and design to your cooking space. Tea towels also make wonderful gifts for your favorite hostess, friend with a new house, or maximalist family member!

FINISHED SIZE: 28″ × 28″

Materials

Blank cotton flour sack towel 28″ × 28″

Speedball Fabric Block Printing Inks in Magenta, Orange, and Yellow

Speedy-Carve block at least 5″ × 5″

Brayer

Ink tray

Iron

Yardstick or ruler

Rainbow Sun Block template (see Templates, page 124)

NOTE ON MATERIALS

There are a lot of different options for blank tea towels, so find one that is 100% cotton, with a smooth finish (not a textured or waffle weave towel). Typically flour sack towels are the best option for block printing, and they work great in the kitchen.

PREPARE THE TOWEL

1 Machine wash the towel on a cold, delicate cycle and tumble dry on low heat. This will remove any dirt, oil, or starch from the cotton and allow the ink to fully adhere to the fabric.

2 Iron the towel on a cotton setting with steam. Be sure to remove all wrinkles, as this can affect the printing process. Lay the towel on your printing surface.

PRINT THE TOWEL

1 Transfer the Rainbow Sun Block template to the Speedy-Carve block (see Transferring Designs, page 25). Carve the block (see Carving Blocks, page 27).

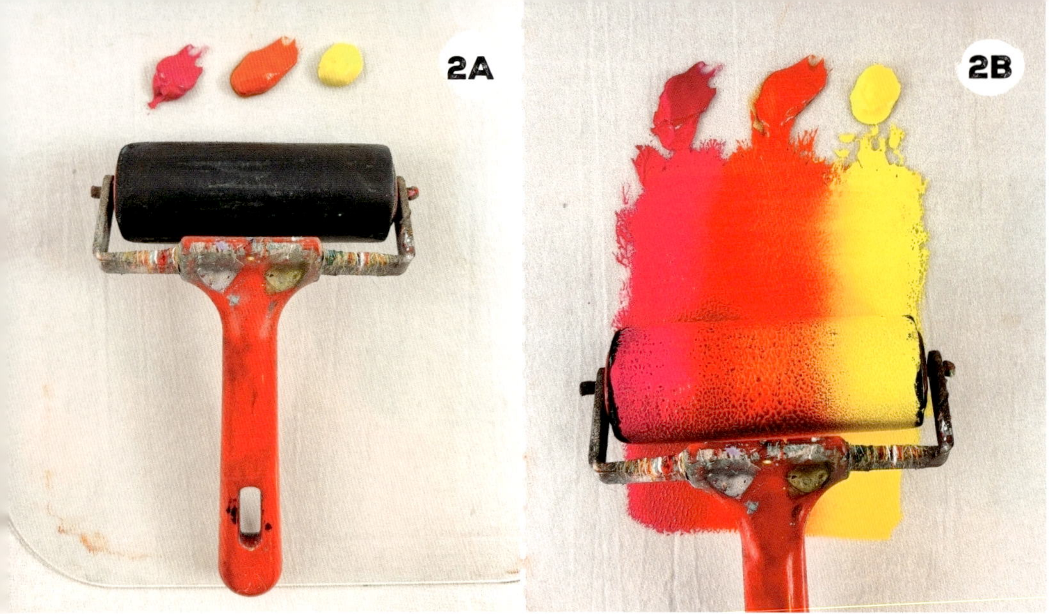

2 Squeeze a small dot of the magenta ink onto the printing tray. Squeeze a dot of the orange next to the magenta, and a dot of yellow next to the orange. Dip the brayer in all 3 colors at once, and roll it on the tray just below the three dots of ink. Continue rolling the ink parallel to the edges of the ink tray, lifting the brayer in between each roll. As you roll the ink, it will start to blend where the colors meet. Each time the brayer needs more ink, dip it in the 3 dots and roll the rainbow in the space below on the ink tray (see Rainbow Rolls, page 32).

3 Roll the ink onto half of the carved block, with the magenta in the middle of the block and the yellow on the edge. Flip the block and repeat, again keeping the magenta in the middle of the block.

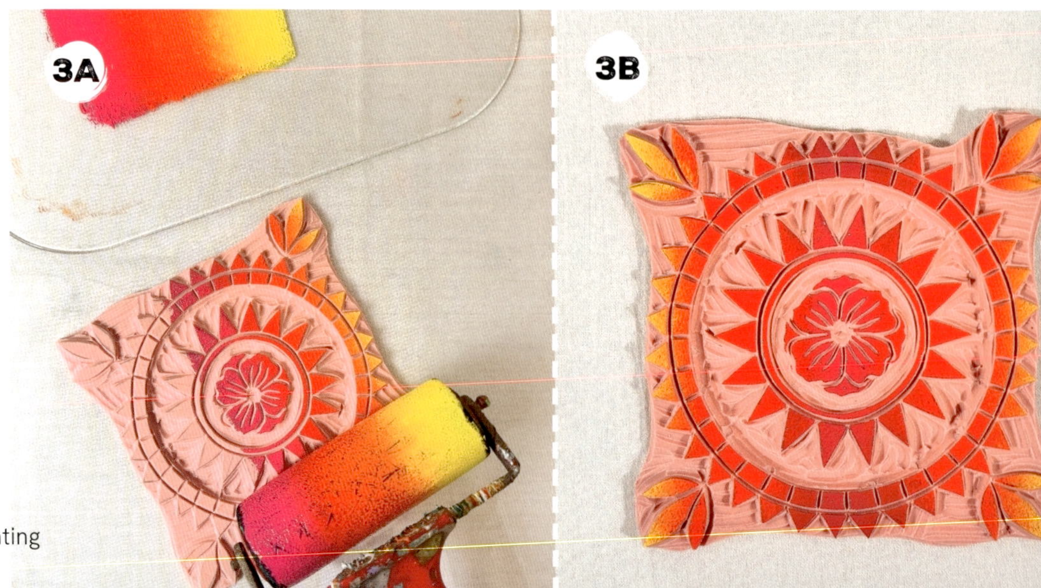

4 Beginning in the bottom left corner of the tea towel, flip the block so it is ink side down, and print in the bottom corner of the towel, all the way to the edges of the towel (see Printing, page 31).

5 Print the first row using the Measured Straight Grid Printing method (page 37). This block measures 5″ × 5″ tall. Print off the edge of the towel if needed, making sure you are printing on a protected surface.

6 Start a new row, continuing to print using the same method until the towel is covered. Again, print off the edge of the towel as needed, including on the top row.

Tip: If you want to balance the half-prints on both sides of the towel, start the first row with the block in the center of the towel, and print toward the edges. Then, the prints will be partial on both edges.

7 Allow the ink to air dry for about one week on a flat surface or drying rack. When the ink has fully dried, the towel is ready. You can machine wash the towel in cold water on a delicate cycle, and tumble dry on low heat.

ORANGES TOTE BAG

You can never have too many tote bags (I say to myself as I walk into the grocery store after accidentally leaving all of my tote bags at home!). A few years ago, Chicago instituted a grocery bag tax, so I try my best to bring a bag or two everywhere I go. Even if your city isn't benefiting from your forgetfulness, it's still great for our Earth to bring reusable totes when you shop! Make a cute one for yourself, and maybe you won't forget it next time.

Materials

Cotton canvas tote bag (any size)

Speedball Fabric Block Printing Ink in Orange, Green, and Magenta

Speedy-Carve block at least 6″ × 5″

3 Brayers

3 Ink trays

Iron

Yardstick or ruler

Heat-erasable pen

Cardboard sheet about the size of the tote bag

Oranges Block template*

Orange Leaves Block template*

Tote Flower Block template*

*For all templates, go to Templates (page 124)

CHOOSING A TOTE

This project works best with a thicker tote fabric; I like to use cotton canvas totes because they tend to wash better, not shrink as much, and the ink typically doesn't bleed through to the back of the bag. However, any cotton tote will work. Just be sure to use a piece of cardboard as recommended.

PREPARE THE TOTE

This tote will be printed using the Symmetrical Pattern Printing method (page 42).

1 Iron any wrinkles out of the tote. Lay the tote flat on the printing work surface. Place the cardboard inside the bag between the front and back layers of fabric.

2 Using the yardstick and pen, measure halfway across the top edge of the tote, and make a mark.

3 Measure halfway along the bottom edge of the tote, and make another mark. Connect the two marks to create a horizontal center line.

4 Measure halfway along one side edge of the tote, and make a mark. Repeat on the other side of the tote. Connect the two marks to make a vertical line, dividing the bag into quadrants.

5 Draw a straight line from corner to corner, creating an *X* on the tote.

PRINT THE TOTE

1 Transfer the 3 block templates to the Speedy-Carve blocks (see Transferring Designs, page 25). Carve the blocks (see Carving Blocks, page 27).

2 Add ink of each color to its own ink tray. Dip the brayers in the ink (one per color), and then roll them on the tray just below the ink dot. Continue rolling until the entire brayer is covered, lifting it between each roll.

3 Roll the green ink onto the carved leaves block (see Inking the Block, page 31). Align the block centered on one of the diagonal lines, about 1″ from the center. Print the block (see Printing, page 31). Repeat 3 more times on the other diagonal lines, as shown.

4 Roll the orange ink onto the carved orange block. Align the bottom of the orange with the top of the leaves, and print an orange below each leaf.

5 Roll the magenta ink onto the flower block. Print one flower on each of the 8 lines, situating the flower about ¼″-½″ from the leaves with the petals facing the perimeter of the bag. Print one flower in the center where all the lines intersect with the petals facing up.

6 Allow the ink to fully dry (about 1 week). Then, iron the design to erase the guidelines. If you need to machine wash the tote, turn it inside out and wash on a cold delicate cycle. Line dry.

JUST PEACHY T-SHIRT

One of my favorite questions from the students I teach is: "I love your shirt, Mrs. Green! Did you make it?" Impress the kiddos (and grown ups) in your life by wearing the cutest peaches and leaves, and tell anyone who will listen that YOU printed your own shirt. And, you don't have to sew to do it! Thrift, shop, or search your closet for a cotton or linen T-shirt and get printing.

Materials

- T-shirt made from a natural fiber
- Sheet of cardboard (about the size of the T-shirt front)
- Speedy-Carve Block at least 4″ × 6″
- Speedball Fabric Block Printing Inks in Magenta, Orange, Turquoise, and Mint
- Brayer
- Ink tray
- Iron
- Yardstick or ruler
- Large sheet of cardboard or cardstock
- Just Peachy and Just Peachy Leaf Block templates (see Templates, page 124)

CHOOSING THE RIGHT SHIRT

Printing on clothing can be tricky depending on what the fabric content is. Choose a T-shirt that is made from natural fibers such as cotton or linen to ensure the ink fully adheres to the fabric and doesn't come out in the wash. This is especially important to pay attention to if you are thrifting the shirt—be sure to check the tags. T-shirts made from polyester or nylon won't let the ink soak in as well. The shirt in this project is 100% cotton.

PREPARE THE SHIRT

1 Machine wash the shirt in warm or hot water with dye and fragrance-free detergent. Using detergents with fragrance or dyes can leave a residue on the fabric that makes it difficult to print. Tumble or line dry the shirt. Iron out any wrinkles on the highest heat the fabric will allow.

2 Put the cardboard sheet inside the shirt, between the front and back layers of fabric. This will prevent any ink from bleeding through to the back of the shirt.

2

PRINT THE SHIRT

peaches

This pattern is randomly printed, so use the Freestyle Repeat Patterns method (page 43). Consider practicing with paper prints if you want to plan the layout in advance.

1 Transfer the Just Peachy and Just Peachy Leaves block templates to the Speedy-Carve blocks (see Transferring Designs, page 25). Carve the block (see Carving Blocks, page 27).

2 Squeeze a dot of magenta ink onto the tray. Squeeze a dot of orange ink right next to it. Dip the brayer in both colors at once, and roll it on the tray just below the dots of ink. Continue rolling the ink parallel to the edges of the ink tray, lifting the brayer in between each roll. As you roll the ink, it will start to blend where the colors meet. Each time the brayer needs more ink, dip it in the dots and roll the rainbow in the space below (see Rainbow Rolls, page 32).

3 Roll the ink onto the carved peach block, making sure both colors blend across the block.

4 Beginning on one shoulder of the T-shirt, print a peach (see Printing, page 31). Repeat on the other shoulder.

5 Begin printing the peach around the shirt, spacing them 2″-3″ apart and rotating the block to print at different angles. Work from top to bottom. Continue printing until you have the desired amount of peaches on the shirt.

6 Leave the ink to fully dry (about 1 week).

leaves

1 Squeeze a drop of turquoise ink onto the tray. Squeeze a dot of mint ink next to it. Rainbow roll the brayer with both colors. Ink the leaves block.

1A

1B

2A

2B

2 Print the leaf print on top of and between the peach prints. Overlap the peaches with the leaves, fill empty spaces, and continue to randomly rotate and place the block. Print until the shirt is filled.

3 Leave the ink to fully dry (about 1 week). Always machine wash on a cold, gentle cycle, and line dry to preserve the print.

CELESTIAL SUNDRESS

Thrifting clothing is fun, environmentally friendly, and a great way to give old things new life. For this project, see if you can find a plain cotton or linen dress at your local thrift store, and with some bright colors and celestial-themed blocks, you can give it a makeover! The colors I chose really pop, but in general, look for a light-colored dress so the blocks stand out.

Materials

Cotton or linen woven sundress

Speedball Fabric Block Printing Inks in Blue and Magenta

Speedy-Carve block at least 4″ × 7″

2 Brayers

2 Ink trays

Iron

Yardstick or ruler

Heat-erasable pen

Celestial Sun and Celestial Moon Block templates (see Templates, page 124)

Sheet of cardboard (about the size of the dress bodice)

NOTE ON MATERIALS

Stretchy or knit fabrics can be tricky to print on, as the fabric can stretch out as the inked blocks are peeled from it and the ink may not adhere as well to the fabric. Try to stick to non-stretch material for block printing.

PREPARE THE DRESS

1 Machine wash the dress in warm or hot water (according to the tag instructions, if applicable) with dye and fragrance free detergent. Using detergents with fragrance or dyes can leave a residue on the fabric that makes it difficult to print. Tumble or line dry the shirt.

2 Iron out any wrinkles on the highest heat the fabric will allow. Lay the bodice flat on the printing work surface.

3 Using the yardstick or ruler, draw a line from armpit to armpit. Make a mark at the halfway point.

4 Using the yardstick or ruler, draw a line from the center of the neckline to the waist. Make a mark at the halfway point. Place the cardboard in between the front and back layers of fabric.

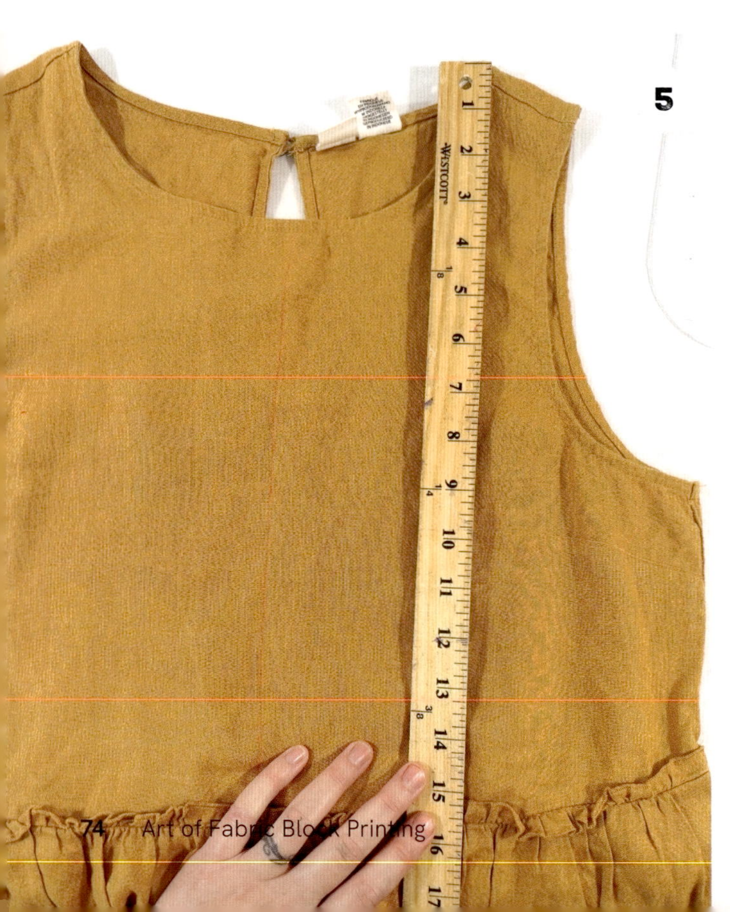

5 Measure from one shoulder seam to the waistline, drawing a mark halfway. Repeat with the other shoulder. If the dress doesn't have a distinct waistline, measure 8″-10″ down from the shoulder seam.

PRINT THE DRESS BODICE

1 Transfer the Celestial Moon and Celestial Sun block templates to the Speedy-Carve blocks (see Transferring Designs, page 25). Carve the block (see Carving Blocks, page 27). The moon is one of the more detailed designs in this book, so move slowly. Carve lines around each of the stars before carving the negative space around them.

2 Squeeze the blue and magenta inks onto separate trays. Dip the brayers in the ink (one per color), and then roll it on the tray just below the ink dot. Continue rolling until the entire brayer is covered, lifting it between each roll. Roll the ink onto the carved block (see Inking the Block, page 31). Roll the magenta ink onto the sun, and the blue ink onto the moon.

3 Using the lines, register and print the moon block in the upper right and lower left corners at the center of the quadrants (see Printing, page 31).

4 Repeat Step 3 in the remaining two spaces with the sun block.

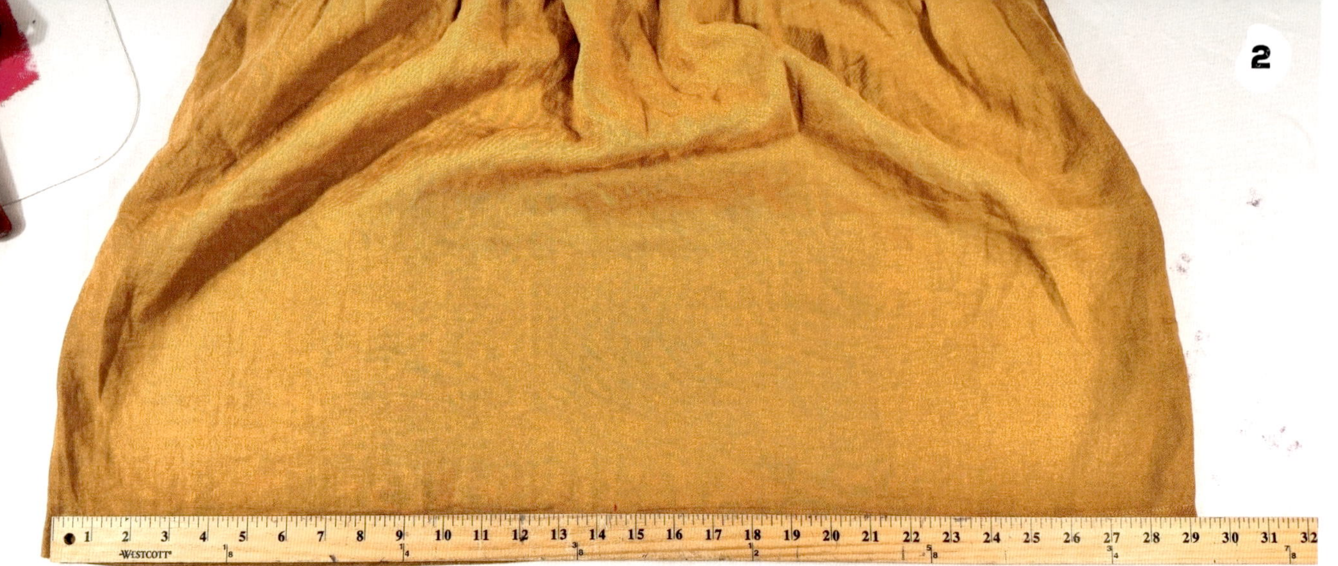

PRINT THE DRESS SKIRT

1 Gently adjust the dress so the skirt lays flat on the work surface. Do not bunch up or wrinkle the bodice, as the ink is still wet.

2 Measure the bottom hem of the skirt, and make a mark halfway. As all garments are a little different, be aware that the exact number of prints that fit on your skirt might not be the exact same number that fit on mine. If needed, adjust the distance between prints to better fit the size of your skirt. My skirt front is approximately 29″ long, and fits 7 prints (4 moons, 3 suns).

3 Print a magenta sun in the center of the skirt, about ½″ from the bottom edge of the skirt.

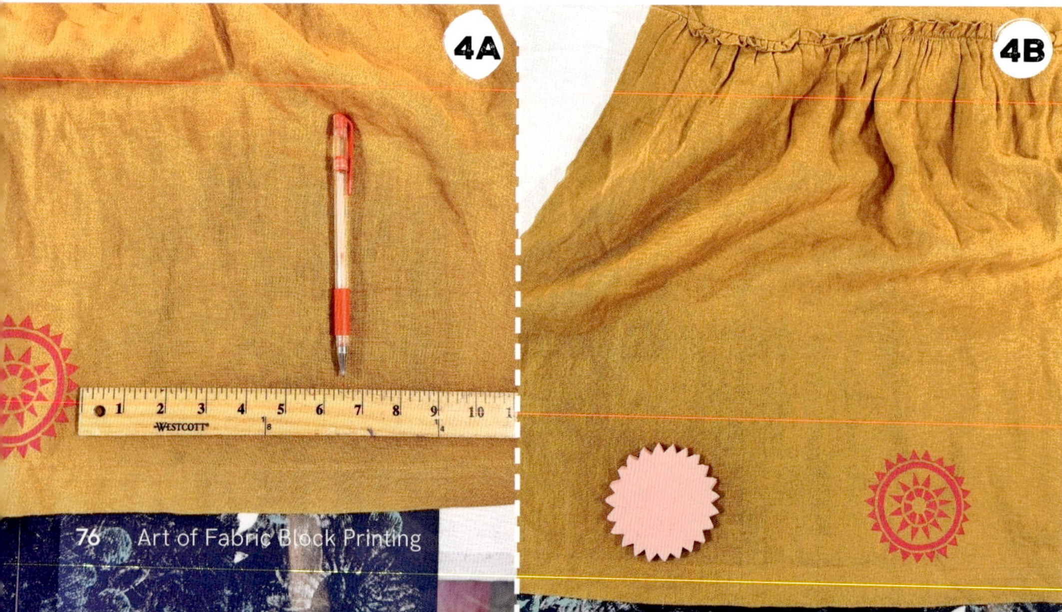

4 Measure from the edge of the printed sun to one edge of the skirt. Mark halfway. Print a sun on the mark. Repeat this on the other side of the skirt (left of center) to make 3 total sun prints.

5 Print a blue moon between each sun print, and on both edges of the skirt.

6 Allow the front of the dress to fully dry, about one week.

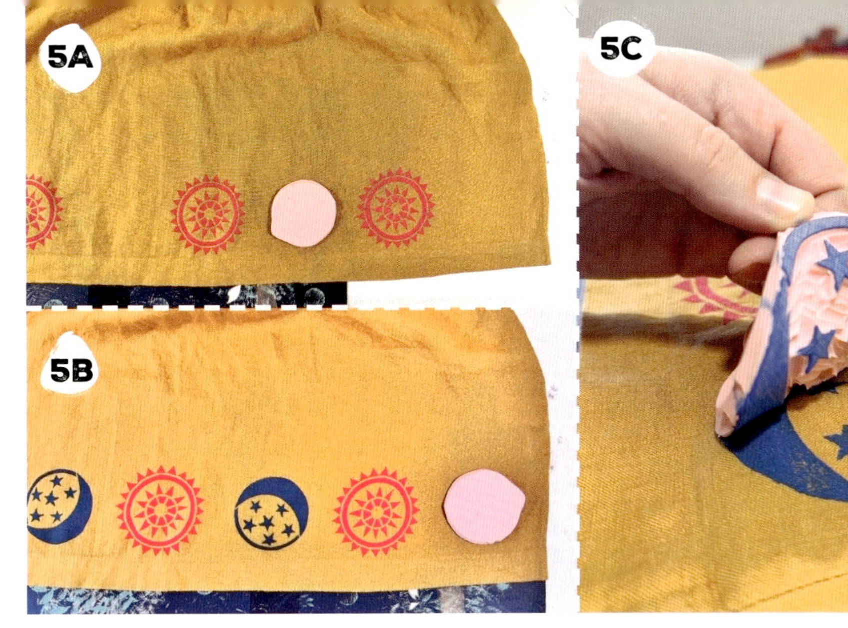

7 Repeat Steps 1- 5 to print suns and moons on the back side of the skirt.

8 Leave the ink to fully dry (about 1 week). Always machine wash on a cold, gentle cycle, and line dry to preserve the prints.

FLORAL VINES BANDANA

Bandanas have made a style comeback in the last few years, giving me flashbacks to wearing them in my hair as a kid! Print your own with a beautiful floral pattern, and use them for more than just hair this time. This size is great for wearing around your neck as a scarf, putting on your dog, or even hanging on the wall as artwork.

FINISHED SIZE: 27″ × 27″

Materials

27″ × 27″ Yellow cotton bandana

Speedball Fabric Block Printing Ink in Mint, Turquoise, Cornsilk, White, and Magenta

Speedy-Carve block at least 9″ × 11″

2 Brayers

2 Ink trays

Iron

Yardstick or ruler

Heat-erasable pen

Stripes Block template*

Flower Block template*

Middle Flower Block template*

Circle Block template*

Vines Block template*

*For all templates, go to Templates (page 124)

NOTE ON MATERIALS

Retailers like Amazon sell great multicolor packs of bandanas. Even though bandanas are easy to sew from fabric, I like purchasing premade bandanas because they come in the classic thin and drapey fabric you expect from a cotton bandana. If you don't have 2 brayers or trays, you can wash the ink off between prints and reuse the same tools. This bandana layers ink, so it has to be printed in 2 sessions.

PREPARE THE BANDANA

1 Machine wash the bandana on a cold delicate cycle, and tumble dry. Iron flat on low heat.

2 Using the yardstick and pen, measure and mark the halfway point on all 4 edges of the bandana. Connect the two opposite marks to divide the bandana into quadrants.

3 Draw a straight line from each corner to corner, creating an *X*.

PRINT THE BANDANA (PART 1)

This project is printed using the Symmetrical Pattern Printing method (page 42).

1 Transfer the 5 block templates to the Speedy-Carve blocks (see Transferring Designs, page 25). Carve the blocks (see Carving Blocks, page 27). When carving the Middle Flower block, make sure to carve away the center negative space so there is a hole in the block.

2 Squeeze the white ink onto a tray. Dip a brayer in the ink, and then roll it on the tray just below the ink dot. Continue rolling until the entire brayer is covered, lifting it between each roll. Roll the ink onto the carved flower block (see Inking the Block, page 31).

3 Align the flower block with a corner of the bandana, centering it on the diagonal line. Print the block (see Printing, page 31). Repeat in each of the four corners.

4 Align the block on the vertical line, just above the center of the bandana. Print the block. Repeat this on the other 3 perpendicular lines, all around the center point. Print another flower, centered on each line, below each of the four center flowers.

5 Repeat Step 2 with the Cornsilk ink and stripes block.

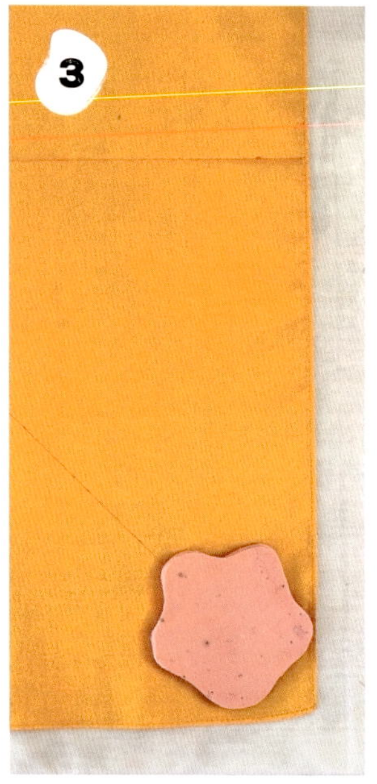

6 Align the stripes block between two corner flower prints, centered on the vertical line, and about ½″ from the bottom edge. Print the block. Repeat on all four edges.

7 Repeat Step 2 with the mint ink and vines block.

8 Center the vines block on one of the diagonal lines, between the corner and center flowers. Make sure the block is oriented so the leaves face the corner. Print the block. Repeat on all four diagonal lines.

9 Allow the bandana to dry completely (about 1 week).

PRINT THE BANDANA (PART 2)

1 Squeeze the Turquoise ink onto a tray. Dip a brayer in the ink, and then roll it on the tray just below the ink dot. Continue rolling until the entire brayer is covered, lifting it between each roll. Roll the ink onto the carved middle flower block.

2 Align the middle flower block with a white flower print, aligning the hole with the center of the flower. Print the block. Repeat on all white flowers.

3 Repeat Step 1 with the magenta ink and circle block. When inking such a small block, it can be tricky to roll the ink if the block is laying flat on the table. Instead, try holding it carefully while you ink.

4 Align the circle block with the middle of a white flower print. Print the circle block. Repeat in the center of each flower. Print a circle in the very center of the bandana.

5 Align the circle block with a line of the horizontal or vertical axis. Move 1″ on either side of the line, between the stripes print and the flower print, and print the circle. Repeat, printing a circle on both sides of each horizontal and vertical line.

6 Center the circle block between the corner flowers and the stripes blocks, about 1″ from the edge of the bandana. Print the block on both sides of each corner flower.

7 Leave the ink to fully dry (about 1 week). Always machine wash on a cold, gentle cycle, and line dry to preserve the prints.

MOON PHASES QUILTED PLACEMATS

Do you have a messy eater in your house? This project is for you! Make your eating space fancier while protecting your table from kid messes (and—let's be honest—spouse messes as well). These placemats have a layer of fleece in them to protect your table from hot dishes. They are also reversible, so you can flip them over! If you want to make them even more special, print fabric for both sides.

YIELDS 2 PLACEMATS.

FINISHED SIZE: 14″ × 18″

Materials

½ yard of Kona cotton in Riviera (main fabric)

½ yard of cotton fabric (backing fabric)

½ yard of Pellon 987 Fusible Fleece

Speedball Fabric Block Printing Ink in White

Speedy-Carve block at least 6½″ × 3½″

Brayer

Ink tray

Iron

Sewing machine

Pins or clips

Heat-erasable pens

Yardstick or ruler

Moon Phases block template (see Templates, page 124)

CUT THE FABRIC

Cut 2 rectangles 15″ × 19″ from the main fabric.

Cut 2 rectangles 15″ × 19″ from the backing fabric.

Cut 2 rectangles 15″ × 19″ from the fusible fleece.

PRINT THE FABRIC

1 Transfer the Moon Phases block template to the Speedy-Carve block (see Transferring Designs, page 25). Carve the block (see Carving Blocks, page 27).

2 Squeeze the ink onto the tray. Dip the brayer in the ink, and then roll it on the tray just below the ink dot. Continue rolling until the entire brayer is covered, lifting it between each roll. Roll the ink onto the carved block (see Inking the Block, page 31).

3 Lay out one rectangle of main fabric. Align the block with the bottom left corner of the fabric, right against the left edge. Print the block (see Printing, page 31).

4 Print the block in a row across the whole bottom of the fabric using the Measured Overlap Straight Grid Printing method (page 38). Align the block against the bottom edge as you go, and print the blocks so they slightly overlap. If necessary, print off the edge of the fabric (protecting the work surface) at the end of the row.

5 Repeat Step 4 to print an aligned row directly above the first row, again overlapping the prints just slightly. Continue printing rows until the fabric is completely covered.

6 Repeat Steps 3–5 on the second rectangle of main fabric. Let the ink dry completely (about 1 week).

SEW THE PLACEMAT

1 Lay down a piece of the fusible fleece, glue side up. Place a piece of the printed main fabric on top, right side up. Iron until the fleece has fully adhered to the fabric. Repeat with the second piece of main fabric and fleece.

2

2 Place a piece of backing fabric on top of the main fabric (right sides together). Pin or clip the pieces together all the way around the rectangle.

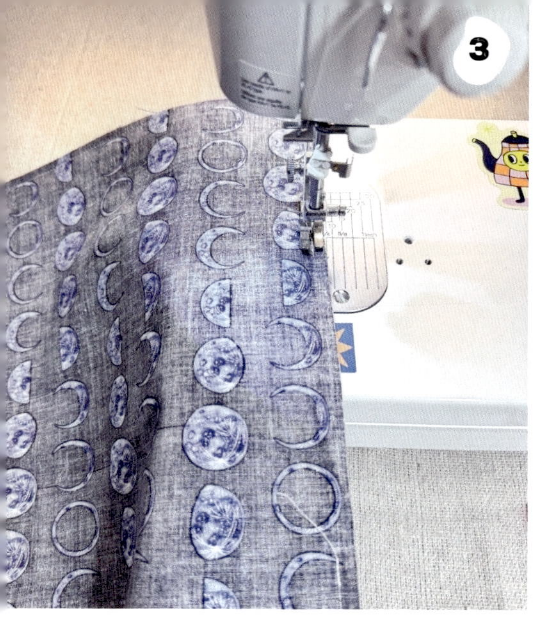

3 Sew along the exterior of the rectangle with a ¼″ seam allowance, leaving a 4″ gap unstitched along the bottom edge. Backstitch at the beginning and end of the seam.

4 Trim all 4 corners, not cutting into the stitches, to reduce bulk. Turn the placemat right side out through the gap.

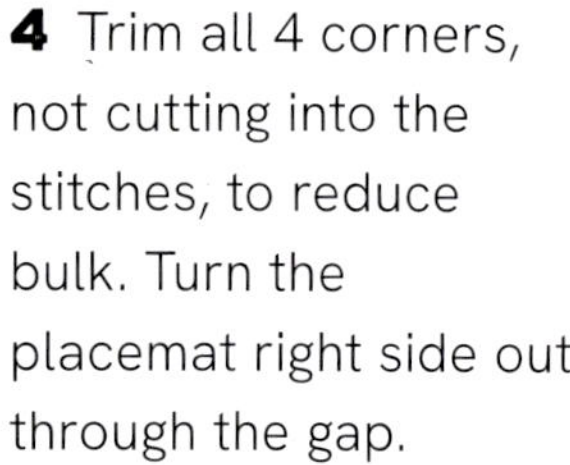

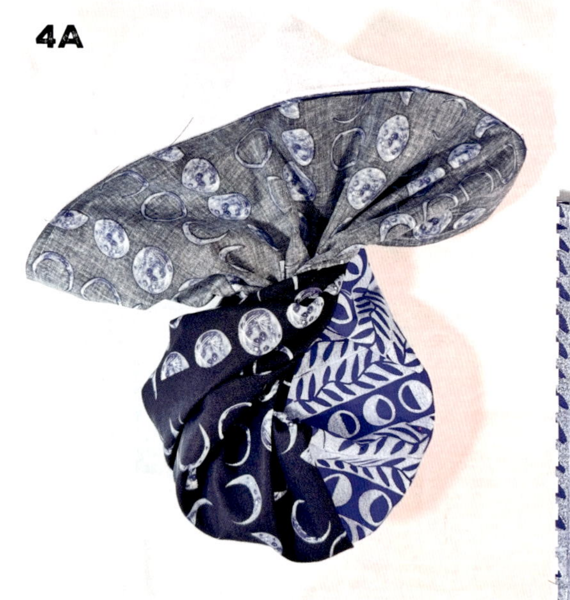

5 Fold the raw edges of the gap in ¼″ to the wrong side. Press. Press the whole placemat flat. Topstitch along all 4 edges of the placemat along the edge, backstitching at the start and end and closing the gap. Repeat Steps 2–5 with the second placemat.

QUILT THE PLACEMATS

1 Quilt the placemats by topstitching them across the whole rectangle. Stitch along each row and column of block prints, backstitching at the beginning and end of each line of stitching, to make a grid design.

2 As needed, machine wash on a cold delicate cycle. Line dry. Iron if needed.

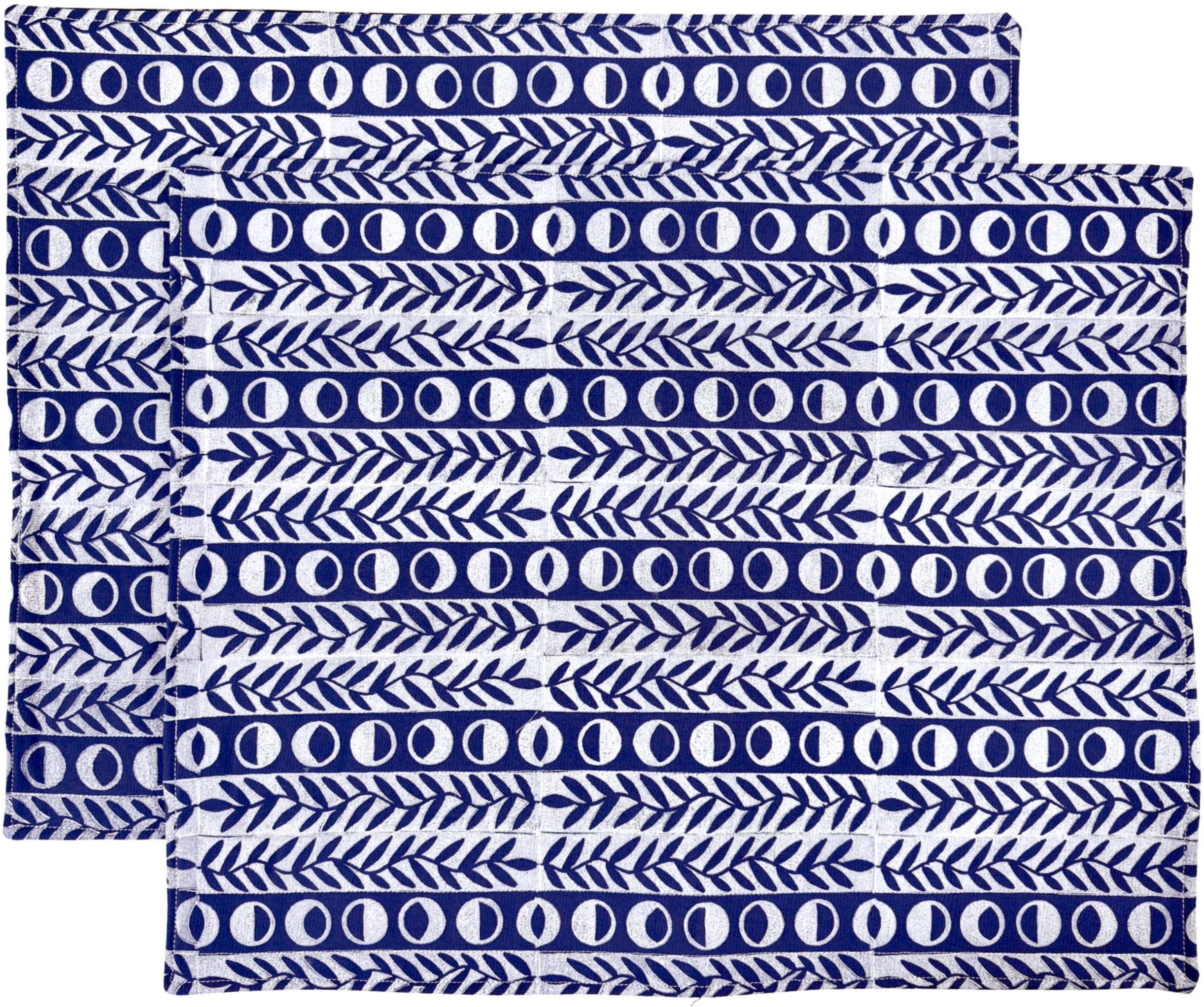

SHINE BRIGHT LIKE A DIAMOND ZIPPER POUCH

A good pouch can be used for anything from art supplies in your child's backpack, to travel necessities at the airport. I love adding interfacing and fleece to my pouches, which gives them enough stability to double as an organizing tool or a going-out clutch! Block printing lends itself so well to hand-painted details, and I am attracted to anything shimmery or shiny. So, to add some sparkle, we are painting each diamond in the print with textile paint.

FINISHED SIZE: 9″ × 7″

Materials

Fat quarter of Kona Cotton fabric in Corsage (main fabric)

Fat quarter of cotton fabric (lining and zipper tabs)

16″ × 20″ piece of Pellon SF101 Fusible Interfacing

16″ × 20″ piece of Pellon 987 Fusible Fleece

8″ zipper

Tassel zipper pull, 5mm jump ring, and pliers (optional)

Speedball Fabric Block Printing Ink in Turquoise

Speedy-Carve block at least 2½″ × 5″

Brayer

Ink tray

Sewing machine with zipper foot

Pins or clips

Iron

Yardstick or ruler

Small flat paintbrush

Geometric Diamonds Block template (see Templates, page 124)

Jacquard Textile paint in Halo Violet Gold

CHOOSING MATERIALS

You don't have to add a special zipper pull if you don't want to, but it really brings your pouch to the next level! I am using a Mini Cotton Jewelry Tassel from Woman Shops World.

CUT THE FABRIC

Cut 2 rectangles 8″ × 10″ from the main fabric.

Cut 2 rectangles 8″ × 10″ from the lining fabric.

Cut 2 rectangles 8″ × 10″ from the fusible interfacing.

Cut 2 rectangles 8″ × 10″ from the fusible fleece.

Cut 2 rectangles 1″ × 2″ from the lining fabric.

PRINT THE FABRIC

1 Transfer the Geometric Diamond block template to the Speedy-Carve block (see Transferring Designs, page 25). Carve the block (see Carving Blocks, page 27).

2 Squeeze the turquoise ink onto the tray. Dip the brayer in the ink, and then roll it on the tray just below the ink dot. Continue rolling until the entire brayer is covered, lifting it between each roll. Roll the ink onto the carved block (see Inking the Block, page 31).

3 Lay both pieces of main fabric flat on the work surface. Press out any wrinkles if needed. Line up the block in the bottom left corner of one rectangle, and print the block (see Printing, page 31).

4 Repeat Step 3, printing the block in connected rows across the whole rectangle using the Measured Overlap Straight Grid Printing method (page 38). Since this pattern requires the prints to touch one another, make sure they line up exactly and overlap just barely. Repeat on the second rectangle piece of main fabric.

5 Allow the ink to fully dry (about 1 week).

4A

4B

4C

PAINT THE DIAMONDS

1 Use the small paintbrush to paint in each of the diamonds created by the connected block prints with the gold textile paint. Completely fill in the diamond spaces, painting carefully. Let the paint dry for about 30 minutes.

Tip: If you're new to painting on fabric, use a piece of scrap fabric as a test. Get used to the consistency of the paint and the texture of the fabric before beginning to carefully paint the printed fabric.

PREPARE THE FABRIC

1 Lay the pieces of fusible interfacing (glue side down) on the wrong side of the printed main fabric. Align the rectangles, then iron the interfacing to the fabric as directed by the manufacturer.

2 Lay the pieces of fusible fleece glue side up. Place the printed main fabric rectangles (right side up) on top, and fuse the fleece to the wrong (interfaced) side of the printed main fabric rectangles with the iron as directed by the manufacturer.

PREPARE THE ZIPPER

1 Fold the zipper tab 1″ × 2″ rectangles in half (to make 1″ × 1″ squares), and press with the iron.

2 Unfold the units from Step 1, and fold both 1″ ends toward the middle crease. Press. Fold along the middle fold again, and press, enclosing the raw ends.

3 Sandwich the ends of the zipper inside the folded zipper tabs. Pin or clip. Sew both tabs in place with the zipper foot. Trim any excess fabric.

SEW THE POUCH

1 Align a 10″ edge of one rectangle of printed main fabric with the closed zipper (right sides together). Center the zipper on the edge. Place one rectangle of lining fabric (right side down), on top of the zipper, aligning both fabric rectangles. Pin or clip together.

2 Sew along the 10″ edge with the zipper foot, attaching the zipper to both rectangles of fabric and going over both zipper tabs. Backstitch at both ends.

3 Fold the outer and lining fabrics so they are wrong sides together, and press with the iron. Topstitch along the edge of the zipper.

4 Place the other piece of printed main fabric right sides together with the other side of the closed zipper (on a 10″ edge of the rectangle). Place the remaining lining fabric, wrong side up, on top of the printed main fabric and zipper. Pin or clip together.

5 Sew along the 10″ edge with the zipper foot, attaching the zipper to both rectangles of fabric and going over both zipper tabs. Backstitch at both ends.

6 Fold the outer and lining fabrics so they are wrong sides together, and press with the iron. Top stitch along the edge of the zipper.

7 Unzip the zipper about halfway. Fold the pouch so that the two rectangles of printed main fabric are right sides together and the lining rectangles are right sides together. Pin or clip together.

7

9

8 Sew along all of the edges of the pouch, leaving a 6″ opening unsewn on the bottom edge of the lining.

9 Turn the pouch right side out through the opening in the lining.

10 Fold the raw edges of the lining opening in toward the wrong side of the fabric by ¼″. Press with the iron. Edgestitch the gap closed along the folds. Push the lining into the pouch, pushing out the corners and zipper tabs.

attach the zipper pull tassel (optional)

1 Open a jump ring with the pliers. Hook the jump ring through the hole of the zipper pull. Place the tassel on the jump ring.

2 Close the jump ring with the pliers.

1

2

TULIPS TABLE RUNNER

Table runners are such a beautiful way to make any dining table fancy, but they can be used for so much more. Try this table runner on your TV stand, on your dresser to brighten up your bedroom, or even hung on the wall as a statement art textile!

FINISHED SIZE: 18″ × 72″

Materials

2¼ yards of Kona Cotton fabric in Pomegranate (main fabric)

Speedball Fabric Block Printing Inks in Lilac, Turquoise, and Blue

Speedy-Carve block at least 8½″ × 7″

3 Brayers

3 Ink trays

Sewing machine

Pins or clips

Iron

Yardstick or ruler

Permanent marker

Tulip block template*

Stem block template*

Triangles and Circles block template*

*For all templates, go to Templates (page 124)

CUT THE FABRIC

Cut 1 rectangle 18″ × 75″ from the main fabric.

cutting note

If you want to buy less fabric, you can also cut smaller rectangles and piece (sew) them together to make a final rectangle size of 18″ × 75″.

HEM THE RUNNER

1 Fold a 75″ edge of the fabric to the wrong side by ½″. Press. Fold again, enclosing the raw edge, and press. Repeat on the other 75″ edge, and then on both 18″ edges.

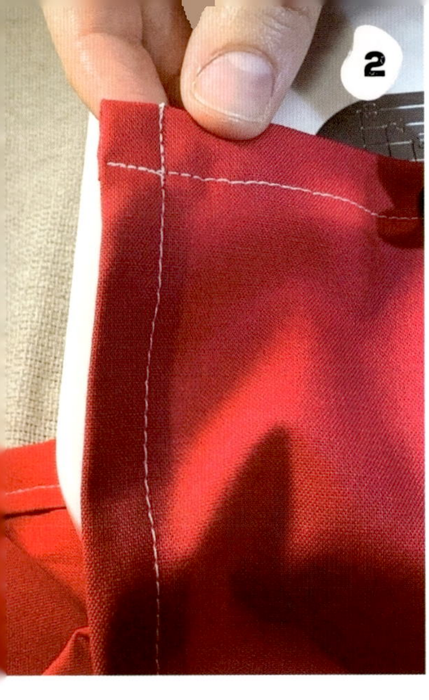

2 Sew the 4 folded hems down along the edge of the folds, starting on one long edge, and backstitching at the beginning and end. Sew all the way from edge to edge, creating a corner square where the stitching intersects.

3 Fold the runner in half, long sides together, and press, creating an ironed crease in the center for printing reference.

PRINT THE RUNNER

1 Transfer the 3 block templates to the Speedy-Carve blocks (see Transferring Designs, page 25). Carve the blocks (see Carving Blocks, page 27).

2 On the backside of the stem and tulip blocks, mark the center of the blocks with the marker. When printing, use these marks to align the center of the stem with the center of the flower.

3 Add ink of each color to its own ink tray. Dip the brayers in the ink (one per color), and then roll it on the tray just below the ink dot. Continue rolling until the entire brayer is covered, lifting it between each roll.

4 Roll the lilac ink onto the carved Tulip block (see Inking the Block, page 31). Align the edge of the block with the stitching on one short edge of the runner. The bottom of the flower should be lined up with the middle crease. Print the tulip (see Printing, page 31).

5 Roll the turquoise ink onto the carved Stem block. Line up the edge of the block with the stitching on the same short edge of the runner, and the mark on the back of the block with the center bottom of the flower. Print the stem.

6 Ink and print the tulip again, about ½″ from the previous print, this time on the other side of the middle crease. The bottom of the flower should still rest against the crease. Ink and print the stem below the flower, again aligning the mark with the middle of the flower.

7 Repeat Step 6 to make 2 more prints of the tulip and stems, alternating the orientation around the fold.

8 Roll the blue ink onto the carved Triangles and Circles block. Center the block between a long edge and the flower prints, approximately 2″ from the hemmed edge. The short side of the block should align with the short edge of the runner, over the hem stitching.

5

6

8

9 Print the Triangles and Circles block (aligned in Step 8). Then, move the block up, keeping it centered, and make a second print.

10 Repeat Steps 8–9 on the other side of the runner.

11 Repeat Steps 4–9 to print the same pattern of tulips, stems, and shapes across the whole table runner. The runner will likely be too long to fit on the printing table, so when you run out of printing space, pull the runner down the front of the table, and continue printing. Print the triangles and circles all the way to the hemmed edge. Print the last flower right before the hem stitching.

Tip: I like to start with the majority of the runner folded at the top of my printing table, and as I work, I pull the table runner down the front of the table so that the fabric is flat, and the ink doesn't transfer to other areas of the runner. However, this means your clothing may accidentally touch the runner as you print, so be sure to wear clothes you can get inky, or wear an apron to protect them.

12 Allow the ink to fully dry (about 1 week). You may need a clothing drying rack if your table space is limited. If you have a friend who can help you move the runner to a rack, that's best!

STRAWBERRY MOON THROW PILLOW

One of the best ways to decorate for each season is with a good throw pillow. They really tie the room together! This one is perfect for summertime, with juicy strawberries and bright red fabric. This pillow is also reversible! Choose a fun backing, and switch up whenever you want. The cherry fabric I use was thrifted, but any cotton canvas will work. And the best part: the cover has a zipper, so when messy little hands or dog paws get on it, you can just throw it in the wash.

FINISHED SIZE: 16″ × 16″

Materials

½ yard of cotton or linen fabric in red (main)

½ yard of cotton canvas (backing)

12″ invisible zipper

16″ x 16″ pillow insert

Speedball Fabric Block Printing Ink in White

Speedy-Carve block at least 4½″ × 4½″

Brayer

Ink tray

Heat-erasable fabric pens

Ruler

Pins or fabric clips

Sewing machine with zipper foot

Seam ripper

Iron

Yardstick or ruler

Strawberry Moon Block template (see Templates, page 124)

Cut the Fabric

Cut 1 square 17″ × 17″ from the main fabric.

Cut 1 square 17″ × 17″ from the backing fabric.

PRINT THE FABRIC

Because the printed fabric needs to dry, plan to print the fabric about a week in advance of when you want to sew the pillow.

1 Transfer the Strawberry Moon block template to the Speedy-Carve block (see Transferring Designs, page 25). Carve the block (see Carving Blocks, page 27).

2 Squeeze the white ink onto the tray. Dip the brayer in the ink, and then roll it on the tray just below the ink dot. Continue rolling until the entire brayer is covered, lifting it between each roll. Roll the ink onto the carved block (see Inking the Block, page 31).

3 Lay out the square of main fabric. Align the block with the bottom left corner of the fabric square, and print the block once (see Printing, page 31).

4 Repeat Step 3, printing the block in rows across the whole square using the Measured Straight Grid Printing method (page 37). Print off the edge of the square as needed, protecting your work surface. Allow the ink to dry completely (for about 1 week).

SEW THE PILLOW

1 Lay the backing fabric wrong side up. Draw lines ¾″ from the edges on all 4 sides. On the bottom edge, draw a small mark 1¾″ from each corner.

2 Line up the main and backing fabric pieces, wrong sides together.

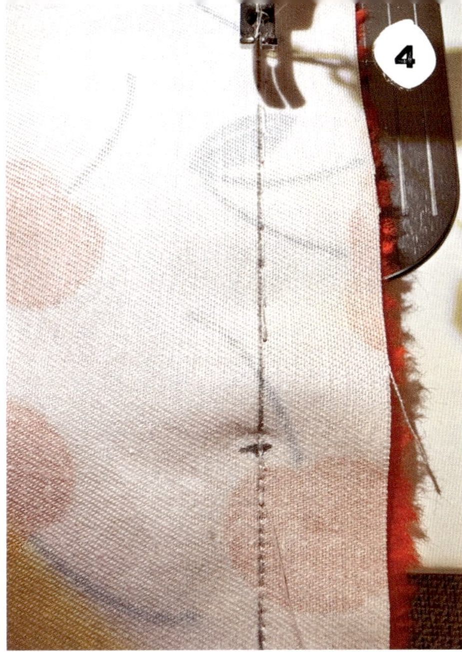

3 On the edge with the marks, sew from the corner to the mark with a short straight stitch on both sides, sewing directly on the line (¾″ seam allowance). Backstitch both lines of stitching.

4 Between the two markings on one edge, sew with a basting stitch as long as your machine allows. Do not backstitch this area; you will be taking these stitches out.

5 Open the fabric pieces flat, wrong side up, and press the seam open.

6 Center the invisible zipper face down on the pressed seam, over the basting stitches, aligning it with the two marks, and pin it in place.

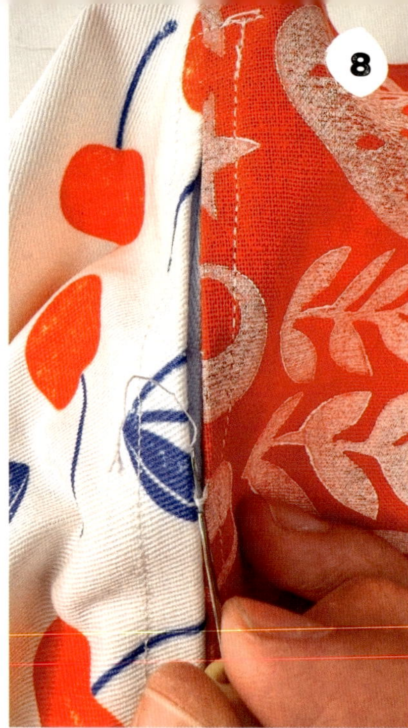

7 With the zipper foot, sew along all 4 sides of the invisible zipper, making sure to backstitch at the beginning and end of each stitch line.

8 Turn the fabric right side up. With a seam ripper, remove the basting stitches where the zipper is. Unzip the zipper about half way.

9

9 Line up the two fabric pieces, wrong sides together, and pin in place.

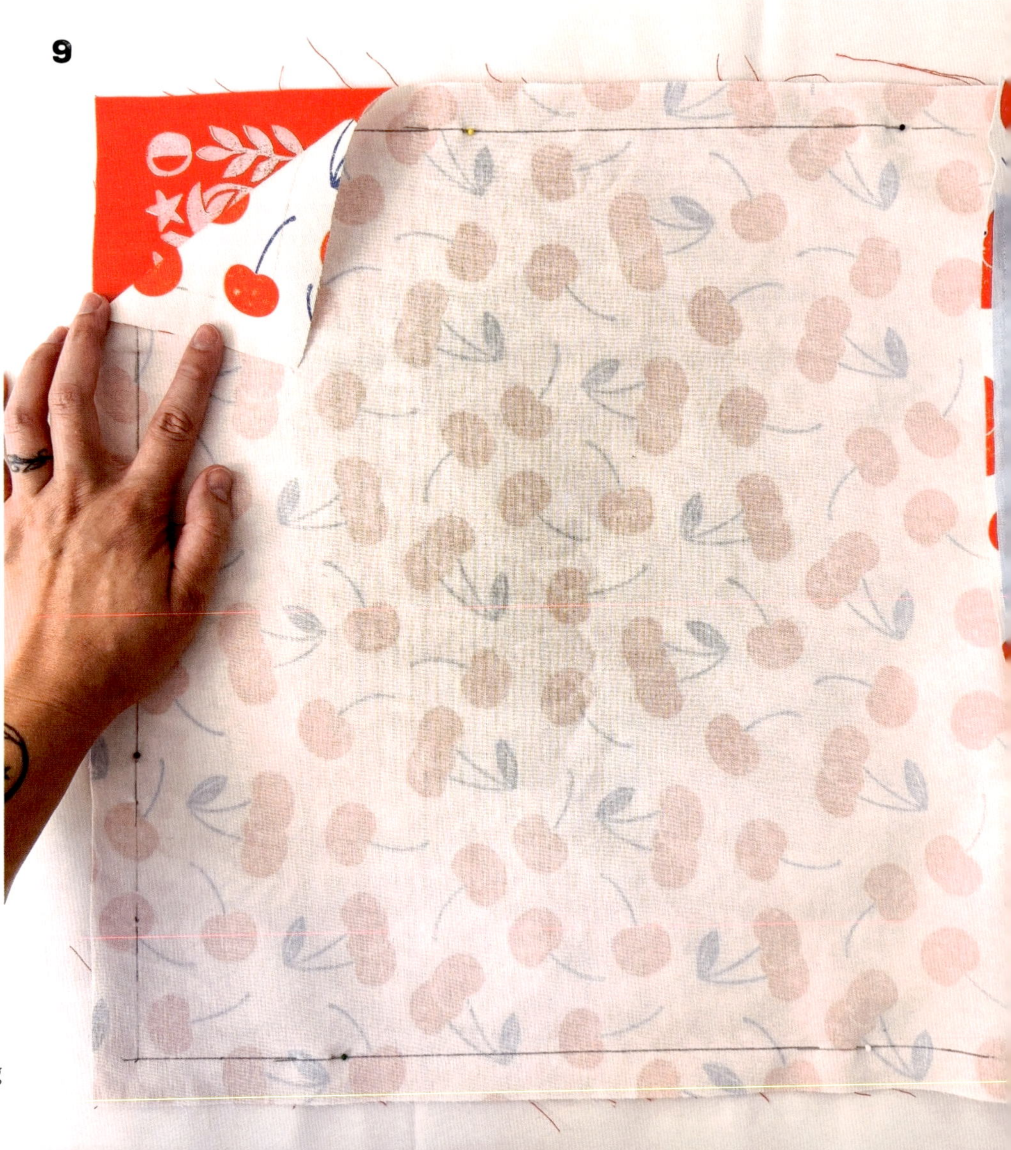

10 Sew along all 3 open sides with a ¾″ seam allowance, backstitching at the beginning and end.

11 Trim the seam allowance to be about ½″ around the whole pillow. Trim the corners at an angle to eliminate bulkiness.

12 Turn the pillowcase right side out, unzip the zipper all the way, and put the pillow insert into the case. Zip closed.

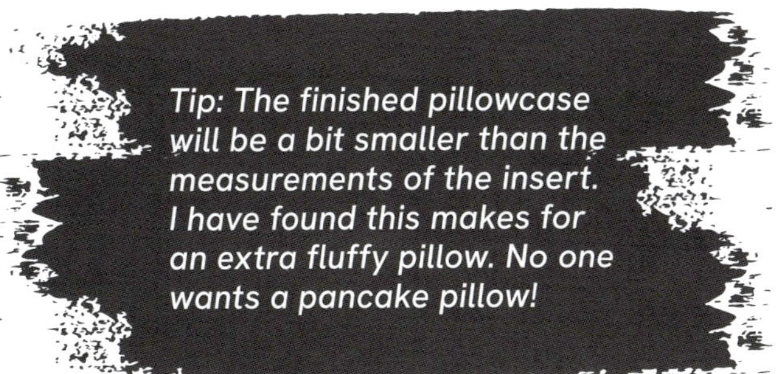

Tip: The finished pillowcase will be a bit smaller than the measurements of the insert. I have found this makes for an extra fluffy pillow. No one wants a pancake pillow!

BLOBBY COSMETICS ZIPPER POUCH

I don't know how mornings work in your house, but here, there is a lot of rushing around, and my makeup ends up strewn all over the bathroom. Keep things a little more tidy with this fun, rainbow printed pouch. It features a boxed bottom, which helps it stand upright and stop things from spilling out of it!

FINISHED SIZE: 11″ × 8″ × 3″

Materials

½ yard of Kona Cotton in Chartreuse (main fabric)

½ yard of cotton fabric (lining fabric)

½ yard of Pellon SF101 Fusible Interfacing

½ yard of Pellon 987 Fusible Fleece

8″ zipper

Speedball Fabric Block Printing Ink in Lilac, Mint, and White

Speedy-Carve block at least 3″ × 3″

Brayer

Ink tray

Sewing machine with zipper foot

Pins or clips

Iron

Yardstick or ruler

Heat erasable pen

Blobs block template (see Templates, page 124)

Cosmetics Bag template (see Templates, page 124)

CUT THE FABRIC

Cut 2 Blobby Cosmetics Zipper Pouch template pieces from the main fabric.

Cut 2 Blobby Cosmetics Zipper Pouch template pieces from the lining fabric.

Cut 2 Blobby Cosmetics Zipper Pouch template pieces template from the fusible interfacing.

Cut 2 Blobby Cosmetics Zipper Pouch template pieces from the fusible fleece.

Cut 2 rectangles 1″ × 6″ from the lining fabric.

PRINT THE FABRIC

1 Transfer the Blobs block template to the Speedy-Carve block (see Transferring Designs, page 25). Carve the block (see Carving Blocks, page 27).

2 Squeeze a dot of lilac ink onto the tray. Squeeze a dot of white ink right next to it, and a drop of mint ink next to that. Dip the brayer in all 3 colors at once, and roll it on the tray just below the dots of ink. Continue rolling the ink parallel to the edges of the ink tray, lifting the brayer in between each roll. As you roll the ink, it will start to blend where the colors meet. Each time the brayer needs more ink, dip it in the dots and roll the rainbow in the space below (see Rainbow Rolls, page 32).

3 Roll the ink onto the carved block, making sure all 3 colors blend across the block.

4 Lay both pieces of main fabric flat on the work surface. Press out any wrinkles if needed. Line up the block in the top left corner of one piece, and print the block (see Printing, page 31). Repeat, printing the block in a row across the top edge, and then a staggered row below using the Measured Staggered Grid Printing method (page 40). Continue printing in staggered rows until the fabric is full.

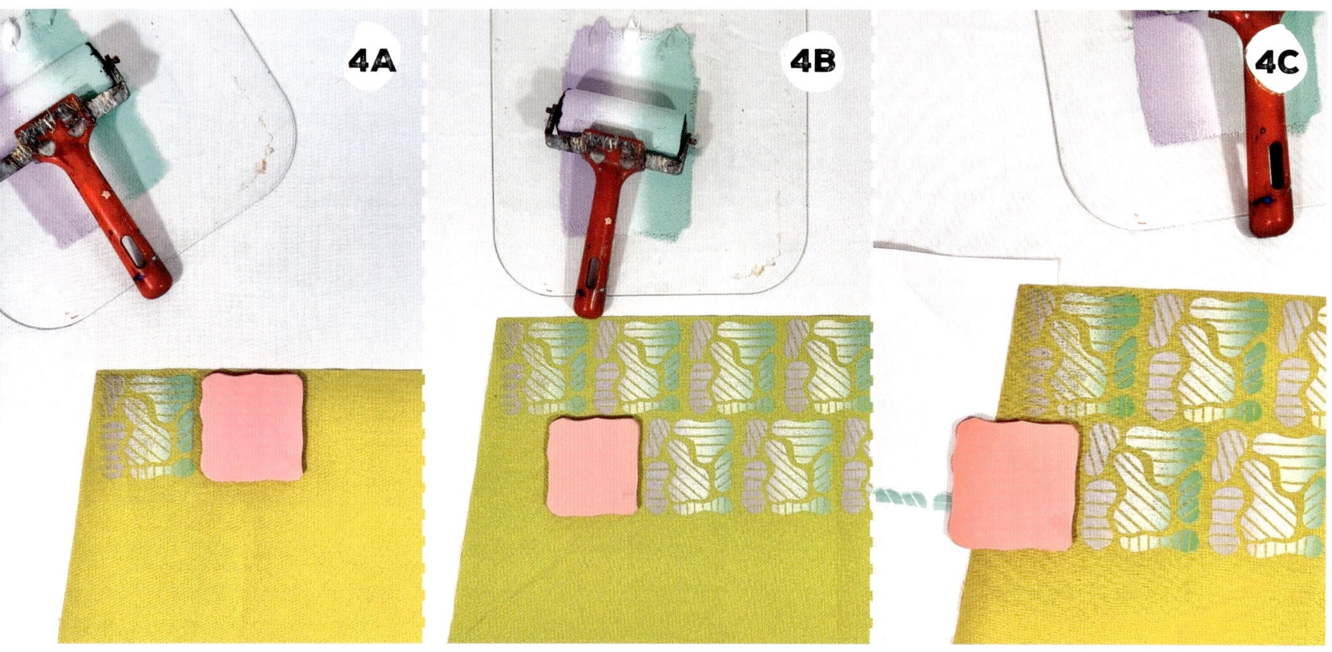

5 As you print the final row, most of the print will go off the edge of the fabric. Allow the ink to fully dry (about 1 week).

PREPARE THE FABRIC

1 Lay the pieces of fusible interfacing (glue side down) on the wrong side of the printed main fabric pieces. Align, then iron the interfacing to the fabric as directed by the manufacturer.

2 Lay the pieces of fusible fleece glue side up. Place the printed main fabric pieces (right side up) on top, and fuse the fleece to the wrong (interfaced) side of the printed main fabric rectangles with the iron as directed by the manufacturer.

PREPARE THE ZIPPER

1 Fold the zipper tab 1″ × 6″ rectangles in half (to make 1″ × 3″ rectangles), and press with the iron.

2 Unfold the units from Step 1, and fold both 1″ ends toward the middle crease. Press. Fold along the middle fold again, and press, enclosing the raw ends.

3 Sandwich the ends of the zipper inside the folded zipper tabs. Pin or clip. Sew both tabs in place with the zipper foot. Trim any excess fabric.

SEW THE POUCH

1 Align the top edge of one piece of printed main fabric with the closed zipper (right sides together). Center the zipper on the edge. Place one piece of lining fabric (right side down), on top of the zipper, aligning both fabric pieces. Pin or clip together.

2 Sew along the edge with the zipper foot, attaching the zipper to both pieces of fabric and going over both zipper tabs. Backstitch at both ends.

3 Fold the outer and lining fabrics so they are wrong sides together, and press with the iron. Topstitch along the edge of the zipper.

4 Place the other piece of printed main fabric (right sides together) with the other side of the closed zipper. Place the remaining lining fabric, wrong side up, on top of the printed main fabric and zipper. Pin or clip together.

5 Sew along the edge with the zipper foot, attaching the zipper to both rectangles of fabric and going over both zipper tabs. Backstitch at both ends.

6 Fold the outer and lining fabrics so they are wrong sides together, and press with the iron. Top stitch along the edge of the zipper.

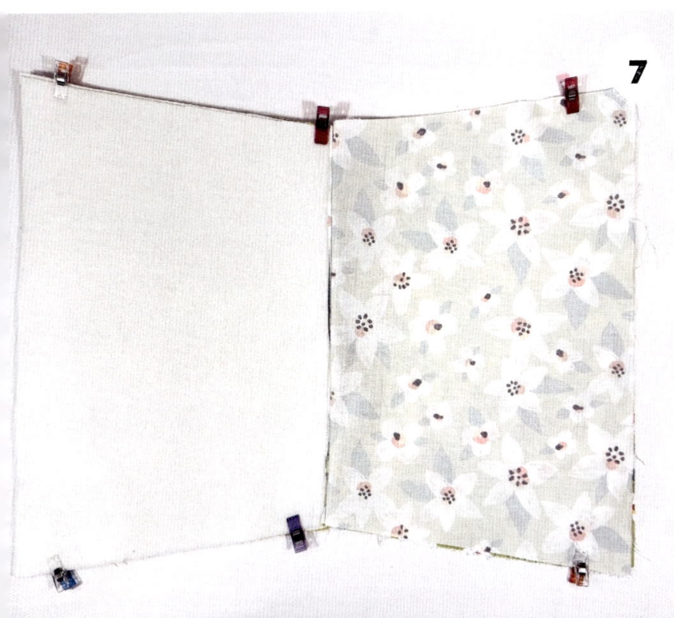

7 Unzip the zipper about halfway. Fold the pouch so that the two pieces of printed main fabric are right sides together and the lining rectangles are right sides together. Pin or clip together.

8 Sew along all of the edges of the pouch, leaving a 6″ opening unsewn on the bottom edge of the lining.

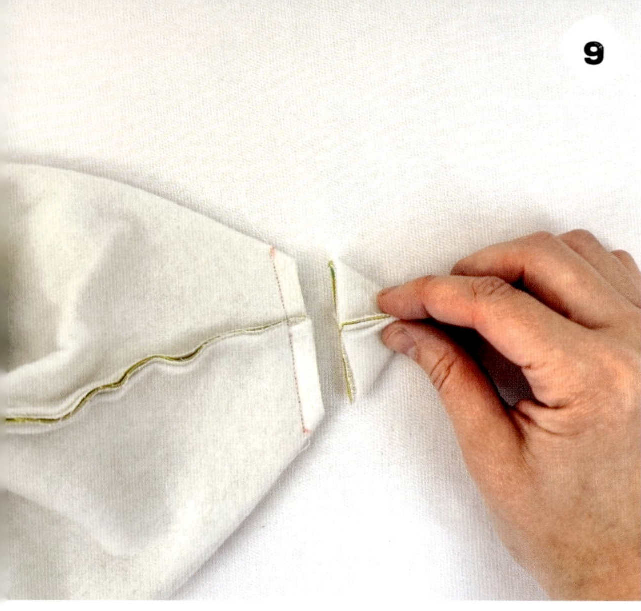

9 Align the side and bottom seams at one corner. Using the pen, draw a mark 2″ from the corner on each side, then connect the marks into a straight line. Stitch on top of the line. Trim away the corner, ¼″ from the seam. Repeat on all 4 corners (main fabric and lining).

10 Turn the pouch right side out through the opening in the lining.

11 Fold the raw edges of the lining opening in toward the wrong side of the fabric by ¼″. Press with the iron. Edgestitch the gap closed along the folds. Push the lining into the pouch, pushing out the corners and zipper tabs.

Tip: To add a little extra sparkle, add a charm to the zipper of the pouch. I found this sparkly smiley face charm at a craft store in the jewelry making section. See the Shine Bright Like a Diamond Zipper Pouch (page 90) for more on adding a charm to the zipper.

FRUITS OVEN MITT

Even the most mundane task of removing food from the oven can be made fun with this bright and cheerful oven mitt! Red fruits on peachy linen gives your kitchen the perfect pop of color. Or, pair this with a hand printed tea towel or apron for the perfect housewarming gift.

Materials

½ yard of Essex linen/cotton in Mango (main fabric)

½ yard of Warm and Natural 100% cotton batting

½ yard of InsulBright insulated batting

½ yard of cotton fabric (lining fabric)

¼ yard of Cotton twill tape for hanging loop, ⅜″ wide (optional)

Speedball Fabric Block Printing Ink in Red

Speedy-Carve block at least 5″ × 5″

Brayer

Ink tray

Sewing machine

Iron

Heat-erasable pen

Yardstick or ruler

Pins or clips

Fruits block template (see Templates, page 124)

Fruits Oven Mitt template (see Templates, page 124)

PRINT THE FABRIC

For this project, I prefer to print first and then cut out the oven mitt shapes. This makes it a little easier to keep the pattern lined up.

1 Lay out the ½ yard of Mango fabric. Iron flat if needed. Transfer the Fruits block template to the Speedy-Carve block (see Transferring Designs, page 25). Carve the block (see Carving Blocks, page 27).

2

2 Squeeze the ink onto the tray. Dip the brayer in the ink, and then roll it on the tray just below the ink dot. Continue rolling until the entire brayer is covered, lifting it between each roll. Roll the ink onto the carved block (see Inking the Block, page 31).

3 Align the block with the bottom left corner of the fabric. Make sure the block is facing the right direction, with all the fruits facing up. Print the block in the bottom left corner, aligning it with the edges of the fabric.

4 Print the block in a row across the whole bottom edge of the fabric using the Measured Straight Grid Printing method (page 37). Align the block against the bottom edge as you go, and print the blocks right next to one another. If necessary, print off the edge of the fabric (protecting the work surface) at the end of the row.

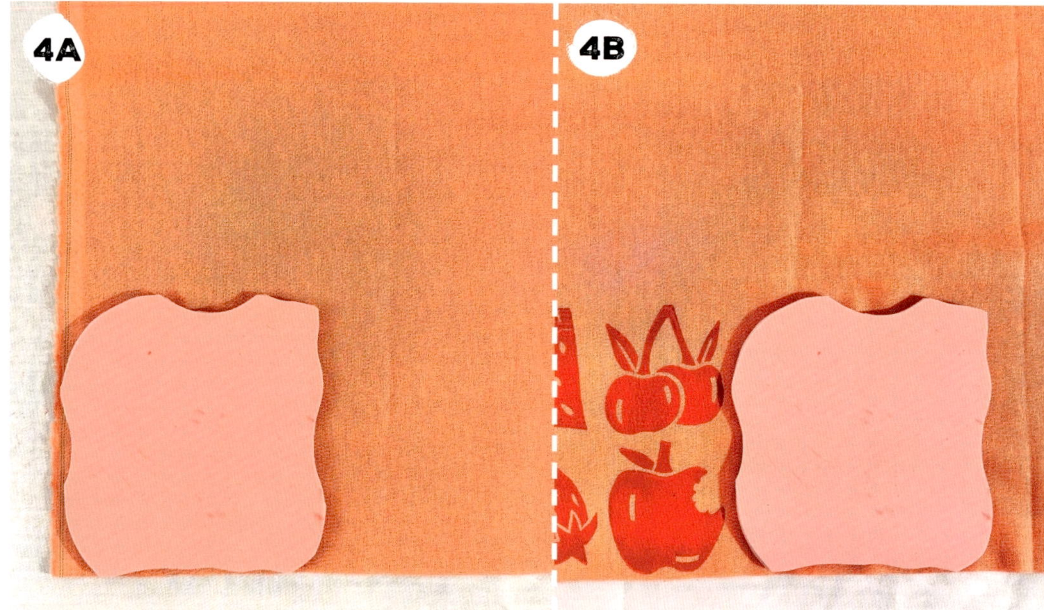

4A

4B

5

5 Repeat Step 4 to print an aligned row directly above the first row. Continue printing rows until the entire fabric is covered. Allow the ink to dry (about 1 week).

CUT THE PIECES

1 Lay the Oven Mitt template on the printed fabric. Trace the template with the pen. Flip the template over, then trace it again. Cut out both shapes.

Tip: I love to save printed scraps for a quilt someday! Any extra printed fabric can be used for a quilt, a pouch—whatever you would like!

2 Repeat Step 1 to cut the mitt template out of the lining fabric, cotton batting, and insulated batting.

3 Cut a piece of cotton twill tape 6″ long.

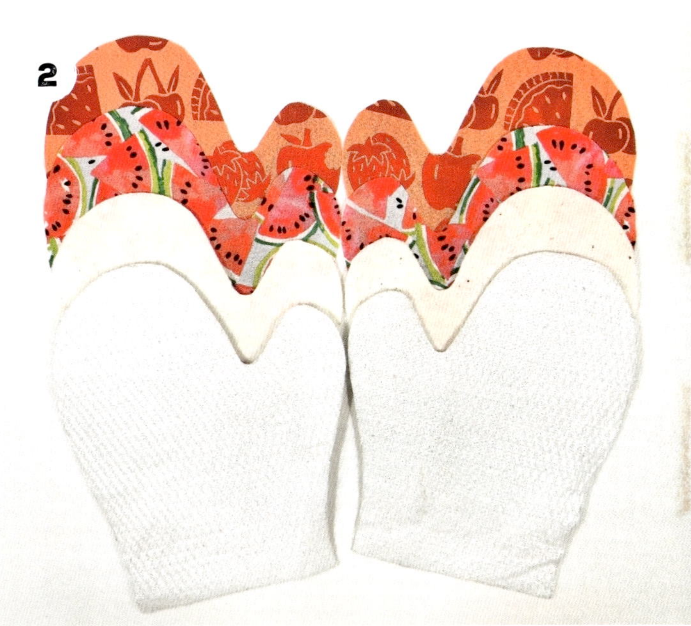

SEW THE OVEN MITT

1 Lay down a piece of cotton batting with the thumb on the right side. Place a matching piece of insulated batting on top and the printed main fabric on top of those. Pin or clip in place.

2 Quilt the three layers together by topstitching over the whole shape. Stitch horizontal lines about 1½″ apart, and then vertical lines about 1½″ apart to make a grid design.

3 If you are including the optional hanging loop, fold the 6″ piece of tape in half. Align and stitch the raw ends of the tape on the side of the mitt without the thumb, about 1½″ above the bottom edge.

4 Repeat Steps 1–2 with the remaining cotton batting, insulated batting, and printed fabric.

5 Line up the two quilted pieces, right sides together, and pin or clip together.

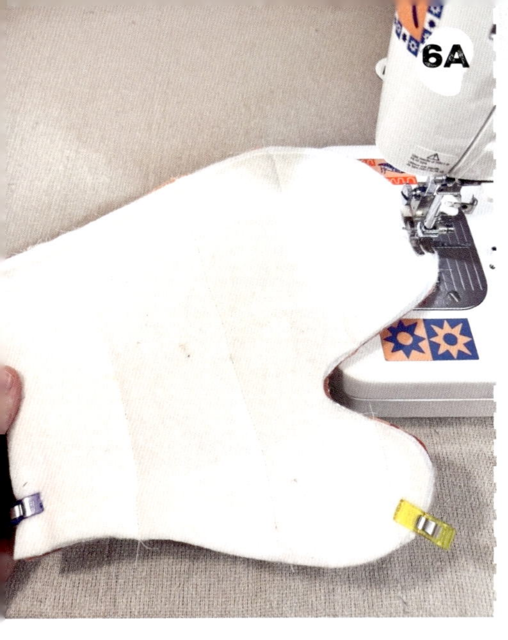

6 Stitch around the exterior of the mitts, leaving the bottom flat edge open. Turn the mitt right side out.

7 Put the two lining pieces of fabric right sides together. Pin or clip together. Stitch around the exterior of the lining pieces, leaving the bottom edge and a 4″ gap at the tip of the mitt unstitched. Backstitch each time you stop and start sewing.

8 Put the lining fabric mitt over the quilted mitt, right sides together. Pin or clip along the bottom opening, aligning the two edges.

9 Stitch the lining and quilted fabrics together around the bottom opening. Pull the quilted mitt exterior through the top opening in the lining fabric.

10 Fold the raw edges of the gap in the lining ¼″ to the wrong side. Press. Topstitch closed along the fold.

11 Push the lining into the quilted fabric mitt. Push out so the shapes are aligned. Iron along the bottom edge, leaving ¼″ of the lining visible from the exterior. Top stitch the bottom opening of the mitt, securing the lining.

TEMPLATES

To access a downloadable PDF of the full size templates, scan this QR code or go to tinyurl.com/11624-patterns-download. For the block templates, all black lines and gray areas should be carved away. All templates in this chapter appear at 50% scale, so should be enlarged before use. All templates in the downloadable PDF appear at 100%.

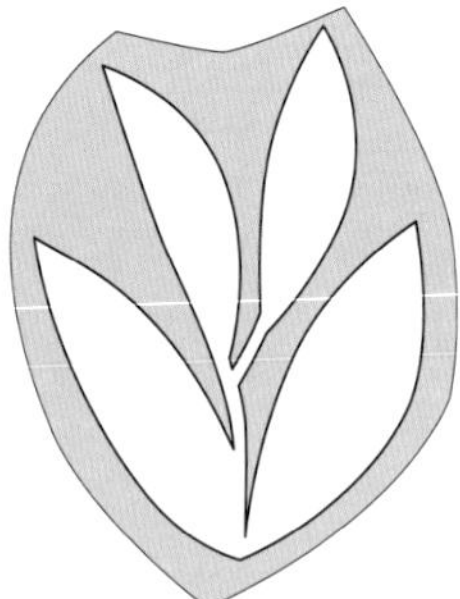

Just Peachy Leaf Block

Moon Phases Block

Rainbow Sun Block

Geometric Diamonds Block

Tulip Block

Strawberry Moon Block

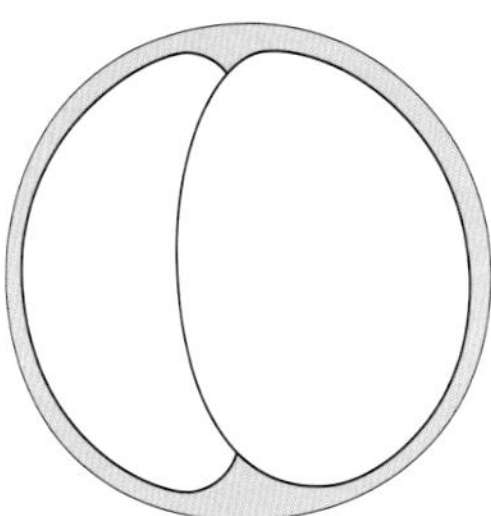
Just Peachy Block

Celestial Moon Block

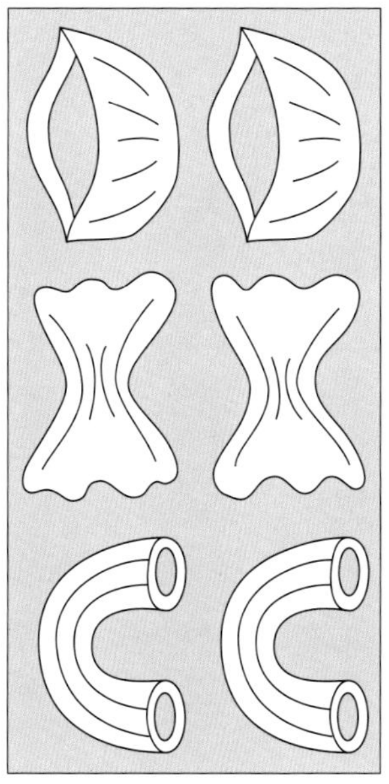
Noodles Block

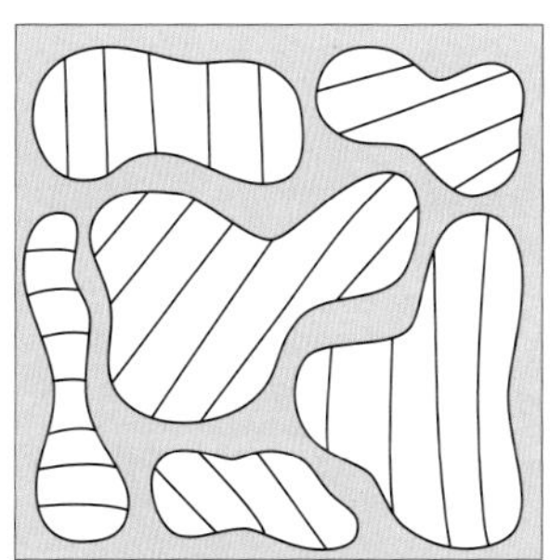
Blobs Block

Celestial Sun Block

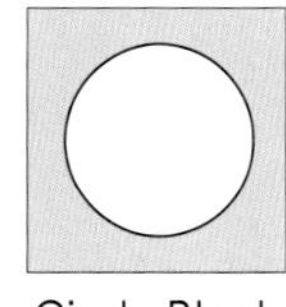
Circle Block

Middle Flower Block

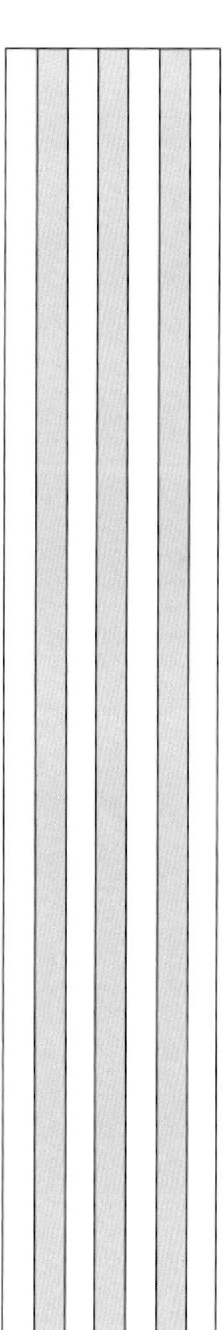
Stripes Block

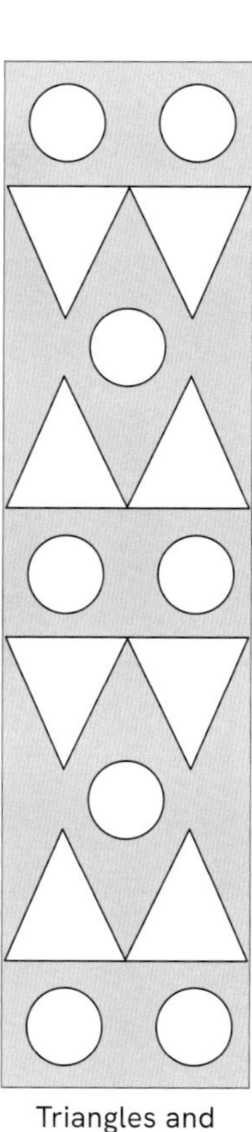
Triangles and Circles Block

Fruits Block

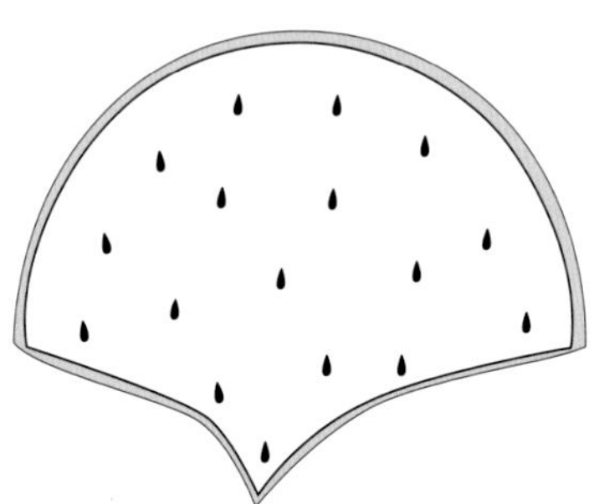
Orange Block

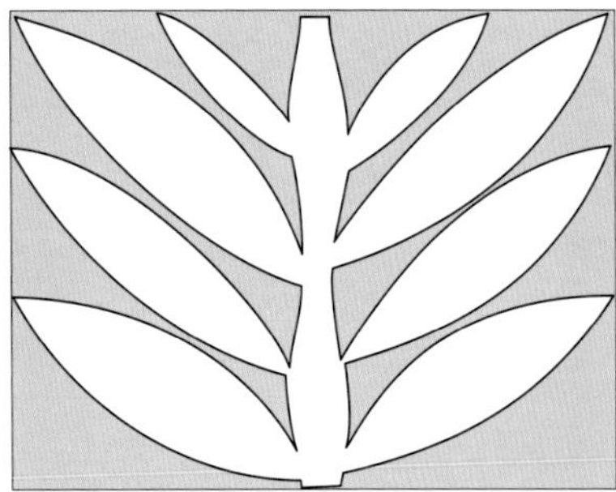
Stem Block

Tote Flower Block

Vines Block

Orange Leaves Block

Flower Block

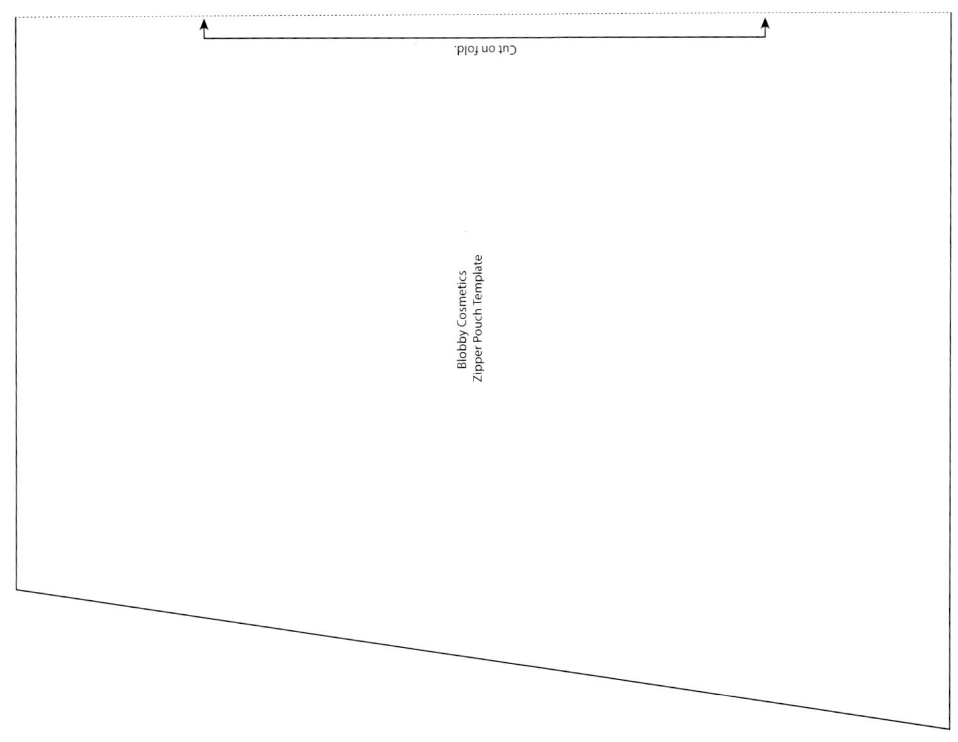
Cut on fold.
Blobby Cosmetics
Zipper Pouch Template

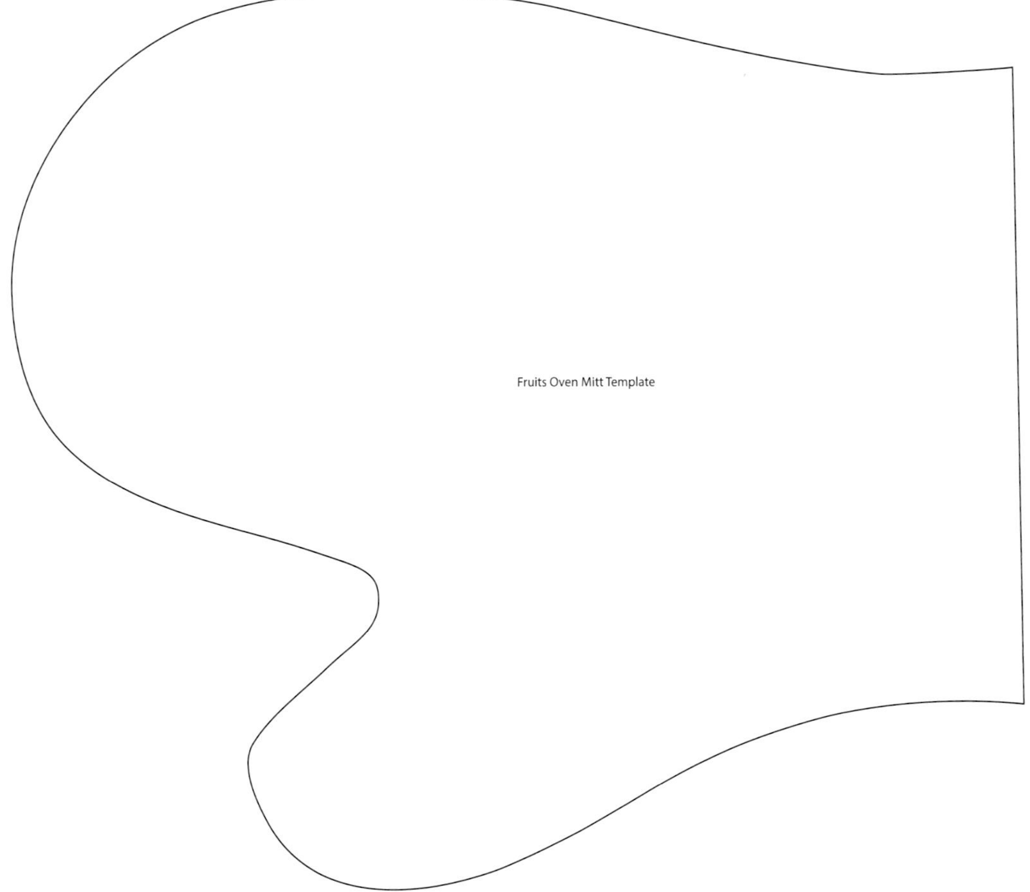
Fruits Oven Mitt Template

ANDRIA GREEN is a midwest artist, illustrator, and printmaker living in the beautiful city of Chicago. She was born in Milwaukee, moved around the Midwest during her childhood, and finally settled into the Chicago area when she was in high school. Her creative adventures began as a child, when she taught herself to cross-stitch ornaments and embroidery hoops as gifts for family members. She enjoyed hand sewing pillows, creating figures out of clay, and making matching jewelry for special occasion outfits. After college, she began nature photography, jewelry making, and watercolor illustrations. However, the two printmaking classes she took in college stuck with her, and she sought a way to put her illustrations to use in creating home goods and accessories.

In 2015, she bought a set of block printing inks and carving blocks, and fell in love with block printing all over again. She loves the hands-on messiness of block printing. Her work has expanded to hand-dyed textiles, sewing, embroidered details, ice dyeing, and the occasional screenprint, but block printing will always have her heart. The simple and rhythmic process of printing repeat patterns has blossomed into an entire product line of towels, napkins, pouches, and more over the past ten years.

Andria began wholesale selling block printed goods to a handful of stores across the country, which has since expanded to over 50 small shops across the United States. She has worked with FabFitFun on an illustrated coloring book, is featured in Botanica by Uppercase Magazine, and has sold at hundreds of art and craft shows. Andria's work has also been featured in an Etsy TV ad and on local Chicago networks such as NBC Chicago and WGN.

Andria's passion for making and creating has also inspired a career of teaching. She began teaching art at her local park district in 2013, and since 2019, has taught art at her son's grade school. Having the opportunity to inspire and be inspired by children on a weekly basis has kept her busy and kept her heart full. Andria always seeks to bring color, life, nature, and whimsy into homes. Andria, her husband, Paul, and their son, Connor, live in Chicago. Her work can be found online at andriagreen.com and on Instagram at @andriafaye